W9-BCB-889

CLASSROOM TESTING
Administration, Scoring and Score Interpretation

CLASSROOM TESTING

ADMINISTRATION, SCORING, AND SCORE INTERPRETATION

CHARLES D. HOPKINS
RICHARD L. ANTES
Indiana State University

120772

F. E. PEACOCK PUBLISHERS, INC.
ITASCA, ILLINOIS 60143

Copyright © 1979
F. E. Peacock Publishers, Inc.
All rights reserved
Library of Congress
Catalog Card No. 78-71815
ISBN 0-87581-244-9

LB
3051
.H7

Contents

Preface

Classroom Testing: Administration, Scoring, and Score Interpretation is the second in a series of books about special topics related to testing in the classroom. The series is intended to serve teachers and preservice teachers with in-depth studies of topics singularly rather than collectively, thus allowing the reader to focus on his/her own present need. We use a "how-to" approach that emphasizes the practical aspects of building tests and the contribution that measures from them can make to strengthen classroom instructional programs.

The material is organized and based on contemporary measurement theory and techniques that have withstood the test of time. A minimum of theory is presented, but the authors feel that a firm foundation of theory underlies the text material. The integration of measurement, ongoing evaluation, terminal evaluation, and further decision making requires an understanding of a certain amount of test theory and is included when deemed necessary.

The practical orientation allows the use of the book in preservice courses which devote a portion of time to testing but more importantly develops a desktop resource for the in-service teacher. The preparation of this book has been guided by the tenet that the preparation of good tests by classroom teachers supports teaching in the classroom and integrates the element of measurement into the educational process. Evaluation of students and programs and decisions made based on those evaluations rely on proper measurement for validity and usefulness in the educational scene. Hopefully, these basic positions are reflected, not only in the material, but more importantly in the classroom programs of those who study from and/or use Classroom Testing: Administration, Scoring, and Score Interpretation to guide test administration, scoring, and score interpretation.

The true measure of the worth of the endeavors of manuscript preparation, publication, and study of a book on testing lies in the impact that is felt in the education, not only of teachers who study it, but also those who are in classes that they teach. If that influence is felt in day-to-day learning activities, then the authors feel that a contribution has been made to the instructional process of education. Since all measurement is only approximate, the measure of worth must remain unknown, as all real-world measurements must be.

C D Hopkins
R L Antes

1 Administration of the Test

The major purpose of testing in the classroom is to measure student achievement as an indication of progress toward educational objectives set for the students. When students know what to expect on a test, they may study accordingly, and, consequently, the objectives for instruction are more likely to be reached. Tests motivate and direct student learning since students base their study of course material on what they expect to be asked to do on tests, and their skills develop accordingly. Because tests guide student learning and help determine how students will prepare for a test, the teacher must capitalize upon the opportunity to develop tests which measure important course objectives. Testing, in this sense, does more than simply indicate how effectively the program teaches what is deemed important: it has a direct influence on what the student learns and the skills s/he develops. Testing goes a long way to determine what students learn and what skills they develop.

Standardized achievement tests are published for class-room use to aid the teacher in obtaining information regarding student achievement in general. **Standardized tests**[1] are based on objectives and curricula from a wide geographical base and are not designed to measure specific objectives and curriculum for a particular classroom. Teacher-made tests are more useful for determining student progress in a particular class. Because the classroom teacher knows what content has been covered and the objectives which have been set based on the needs of a particular classroom of students, the teacher has the best opportunity to construct tests to measure the outcomes of a unit of study or a course. For

---

[1] The first time a term which is listed in the glossary is used in the text, it will appear in **boldface** type. As indicated, use of **standardized test** is described in the glossary.

these reasons a well-planned test program which includes components of both classroom tests and standardized tests is needed.

The results of teacher-made tests are valuable when reporting student progress, evaluating an ongoing program, making an **evaluation** of a completed course of study, and making decisions about promotion and placement for future study. The classroom teacher should be concerned with measuring student progress and should also strive to build tests which motivate and direct student learning as well as provide needed feedback for making decisions about students and school programs. Testing is a structured manner of observing. Observation of current behavior indicates effectiveness of previous instruction, the present status of student development, and aids in predicting future behavior. This book is intended to point up the importance of test administration and test scoring, to provide guidance to proper administration and scoring procedures, and to direct the reader in ways to interpret the obtained scores according to one of two reference systems—criterion referencing or norm referencing.

Importance

Classroom Testing: Construction[2] dealt with the intricacies of testing, especially test construction, up to the actual administration of the test. During the initial construction considerations, the teacher must give attention to important aspects of test administration since the conditions under which a test is administered affect the **validity** of the test scores. A well-constructed and otherwise valid test can have the validity of the test scores reduced through haphazard or careless administration procedures.

Before administering a classroom test, the teacher should have built appropriate instructional objectives for the content covered. These objectives should have been expressed in terms of student behavior. The teacher also should have prepared a **table of specifications,** written items appropriate for the subject matter and desired student behavior, and assembled and reproduced the test instrument with directions for recording the responses. Although the administration of the test may be the simplest aspect of testing, serious consideration must be given to administration procedures to assure that the usefulness of the test is not reduced by lack of attention to important parts of the process. Each teacher has the responsibility to set the stage for test administration by careful consideration of details of psychological aspects of testing, physi-

[2] Charles D. Hopkins and Richard L. Antes, *Classroom Testing: Construction* (Itasca, Ill.: F. E. Peacock Publishers, Inc., 1979).

cal conditions of the room, and other considerations of the actual test situation. Especially important is the establishment of the purpose of the test within the student's mind. If the student feels that information collected by a test will benefit him/her, the teacher can expect more accurate test scores.

The unintentional overlooking of details of test administration may occur most often when teachers who have left test construction to the last minute feel relieved that the test items are completed in time for the test session. On the other hand, teachers who methodically complete test items and the test itself usually deal with test administration in a precise manner. In either case, a review of proper test administration procedures will assure more valid test results since each student will have the opportunity to exhibit true achievement at the highest level possible. The guiding principle in test administration is to provide a milieu in which each student will have an opportunity to perform at his/her true achievement level.

Psychological Considerations

The factors that influence how students are affected by the thought of taking a particular test and their feelings about testing in general are psychological considerations that, when controlled, will support the obtainment of a true measure of student achievement. These factors are an aggregate of emotions, traits, and characteristic behavioral patterns based on each individual's past test-taking experiences. This chapter emphasizes the importance of the early experiences a student has with tests. Nursery school, kindergarten, and primary school teachers should attempt to establish a positive attitude with children to the word "test." When a child's early school encounters with tests are positive, his/her psychological reaction to later test experiences should allow for optimal functioning.

STUDENT BENEFIT

The teacher's actions more than mere words can convince students that tests are given for their benefit. Because tests are given to provide feedback about progress in learning and to direct future learning, the teacher must help each student show how well s/he has met the goals set for each unit of instruction. Students should have time to see and reflect on each item of the test and the opportunity to clarify concerns which are unclear. A cooperative endeavor between teacher and student is essential for best learning progress. Observational procedures, such as (1) **direct observation** and devices to aid direct observation (checklists, scorecards, rating scales, unobtrusive observation, anecdotal records, and mechanical instruments) and (2) **measurement** through use of classroom and commercially published tests, provide information relevant to student progress.

When students have been exposed to good testing practices, many of them are enthusiastic concerning the return of a test and are willing to discuss items which they have missed. Based on student responses to items and their questions when reviewing the test, the teacher can determine those subject topics which need reteaching or where more time is needed for student learning. Teachers have a responsibility to help the less capable student to see positive aspects of tests. A realistic approach to helping a student know his/her potential by understanding strengths and weaknesses through test results allows that student to benefit from the testing session.

OPTIMUM MOTIVATION

Motivation is the state of the mind which indicates when the student is inclined to action or inaction. Students who are internally inclined to action are considered to be intrinsically motivated; they attain satisfaction from merely doing their best in schoolwork. Extrinsic motivation that calls into play the mechanism which stimulates action is necessary for some students. Motivating students is thought of as what the teacher does extrinsically to encourage learner involvement in a particular learning activity. Students possess intrinsic motivation in varying degrees along a continuum which ranges from very little to very much; therefore, any action on the part of the teacher will produce different actions by different learners.

Tests can provide the extrinsic motivation necessary for some students. When the teacher announces a test date well in advance of the test session, most students are motivated to study the material assigned. Announcement of a test well in advance helps set the stage while unannounced or surprise tests may create negative feelings toward the teacher and learning. Periodically administered quizzes over small amounts of content seem to direct students to study consistently and provide incentive for continuous progression. A program of short quizzes, tests throughout the instructional period, and terminal examinations when needed should be an integral part of the instructional program.

Motivation can be kept at high levels by early understanding of how tests are used to support instruction. Using a test as a threat for lack of action on the part of students is not an acceptable way to induce students to study. The instinctive desire of students to know and learn must be capitalized upon by the teacher, and testing can provide the capstone to a rewarding learning experience.

The teacher must interpret success on a test in terms of each student's particular abilities. The teacher must transfer this aspect of success into action by explaining to each student his/her attainment relative to his/her capacity for achievement. Optimum motivation necessitates the report of achievement to students in such a way that each student feels positive about what s/he has learned. Teachers should play down the idea that each student must achieve perfect success on each test while still emphasizing the importance of doing one's best. However, some mastery tests require the student to score at or near perfect performance to direct future learning experiences (see Chapter 7).

TEST ANXIETY

Anxiety is a disturbance of mind created by some uncertain event. Test anxiety is a tense emotional state characterized by fear and apprehension of the testing situation and is usually based upon the fear of not doing well or a feeling of being inadequately prepared. In American culture anxiety is a pervasive factor. Nearly everyone has been affected by some type of anxiety, at one time or another, even though an explanation about what it was like may be impossible to give in detail.

In test anxiety there may be apprehension ranging from uneasiness to fear. Test anxiety is a situational condition and temporarily exemplified by anxious feelings about the test. Effects of severe test anxiety may be recognized when a student's low test performance contradicts other performance demonstrated in the classroom.

Some students who do not perform well on tests blame an anxious feeling, test anxiety, for their poor test scores. They insist that they know more than what their test scores indicate. Although there may be cases where a very high level of anxiety may cause a student to be so fearful that s/he does very poorly, research has indicated that the problem is not as wide-spread as students believe. However, teachers need to understand that while a certain degree of concern by the student may be beneficial to optimum test performance, high levels of anxiety are not desirable. It is possible, based on results of studies of anxiety, to state that a relatively low to moderate level of anxiety may be beneficial to learning and test taking while a high level of anxiety during learning and test taking is detrimental to student performance. High levels of test anxiety can best be controlled by the teacher's care and attention when preparing students for a test situation. This preparation is particularly important for young elementary students since test anxiety begins in the elementary grades. It is generally agreed that the well-informed, best-prepared, capable student feels less anxiety or fear of a test. Teachers at all levels should maintain an atmosphere to keep students in a proper mind set and inform them early about upcoming tests.

Anxiety about or fear of the test situation can be diminished through the development of a positive testing atmosphere. This may be partially accomplished by prior announcements of dates for quizzes and examinations. Surprise or unannounced tests should in the most part be avoided, although there may be an unusual set of circumstances which would support the use of a surprise test. For example, in a classroom where students are not keeping up with assignments or doing the reading, the teacher may mention that there will be a short quiz within the next three days. This should stimulate students to keep up with the assignments, not as a threat, but as a reminder of the student's commitment to learning.

A detailed explanation of the content to be covered on a test as well as specifying the type and number of test items to be given will reduce the surprise element of a test. The teacher may wish to provide examples of types of items as they relate to the content to be covered. It is recommended that early in the school year the teacher administer a brief test, the results of which will not be recorded. The administration is for student practice and allows student exposure to a few typical items which illustrate what students can expect. Students may study differently for **selection-type items** (true-false, multiple-choice, matching, and classification), **supply-type items** (completion, short-answer, and essay), and **problem-type items** (mathematical and technical).[3] Even if students do not study differently for different types of items, good feelings are created in their minds when they have been informed that the test consists of so many multiple-choice and essay items, or whatever combination of items is to be presented on the test.

Students should be informed that sufficient time will be allowed for completion of the test and that while some students will complete the test prior to others, everyone should be able to work through all items. The amount of credit given for each item on the test and the part of the total score represented by each test task are important facts for students to know prior to taking a test. Information presented during discussion of testing is usually presented to the students during the first few days of a new school year, but it needs to be reviewed at test time. The teacher should point out that adequate preparation for a test will eliminate much of the anxiety one may feel. The teacher should supply each student with his/her own copy of the test items whenever tests are administered. Some special use may be found for an unorthodox way of

---

[3] A thorough discussion of each type of test item can be found in Charles D. Hopkins and Richard L. Antes, *Classroom Measurement and Evaluation.* (Itasca, Ill.: F. E. Peacock Publishers, Inc., 1978).

test presentation, such as using slides to project the items on a screen or writing the items on the chalkboard, but these approaches should be used cautiously. By returning test results promptly and providing students with an opportunity to go over the test items, the teacher supports the earlier statements that tests are given for students' benefit. The teacher who has established a good rapport with students and is aware of their special needs and concerns can provide a testing session that will afford the optimum level of anxiety to work for instructional progress and alleviate any high levels of anxiety. When test administration considerations are attended to, students get the feeling that tests are really given for their benefit.

TEST-TAKING SKILL

Test-taking skill refers to how well a student understands and can cope with the demands of a testing session. Since some students may be more highly skilled in taking tests than others, test scores are likely to vary accordingly. To overcome these inequities the teacher should provide all students with the information and training they need to become skilled test takers thus equating the contribution of test taking skill to the final test measures. Some considerations concerning the test situation to be presented to students are:

1. **Be mentally and physically fresh for a test by getting a good rest the night before a test.**
2. **Follow directions exactly. Make sure that directions are re-read and procedures understood. Listen intently when any student asks a question or requests clarification of directions during testing.**
3. **Skim the entire test to determine the types of items being presented and the approximate amount of time necessary for responding to each section and the entire test.**
4. **When taking the test, mark any items skipped or items which need further deliberation.**
5. **When responding to selection-type items, attempt to eliminate any alternative which can be identified as incorrect when you are not sure about the correct response.**
6. **When responding to essay items, plan the response by outlining and ordering the points you wish to make.**
7. **Use the time allotted for testing wisely.**
8. **When time is available, check each response to make sure that the recorded response is the chosen response.**

These and any additional considerations the teacher may have should be discussed periodically until all students know how to take tests effectively.

A **test-wise** student may be able to respond correctly to some items without knowledge about the subject content, thereby receiving a higher raw score on the test than a student who is more knowledge-able in the subject content but lacks the test-wiseness. The advantage a test-wise student has can be reduced by the teacher's careful attention in early review of each item to determine if any of the clues test-wise students pick up are included in the items for a test. If there are items which have defects, those items can be rewritten to eliminate the clues.

Based on the degree to which the item writer fails to incor-porate general guides and specific item-writing considerations, clues to the correct response may be provided by the way an item is presented.[4] When the student uses his/her knowledge of test items to identify the shortcomings of items, the student becomes test-wise. The advantage that a test-wise student has can be reduced to a minimum by considering the following points when preparing test items:

1. **When blanks of different sizes appear in completion items, the approximate length of the word may be indicated, thus eliminating words of certain lengths.**
2. **Wording of a test item may imply that either a singular or plural word be supplied, thus eliminating some alternatives.**
3. **Wording of a test item may imply that the correct response begins with a vowel or consonant, thus eliminating some alternatives.**
4. **True items may be longer than false items because they require qualifying phrases.**
5. **Words such as "always," "never," "all," "none" are associated with false items.**
6. **Words such as "usually," "often," "may" are associated with true items.**
7. **More false than true statements may be included on the test to provide higher discrimination.**
8. **Some alternatives in a multiple-choice item may not be parallel with the other alternatives.**
9. **An incomplete statement may have one or more distracter alternatives which are not parallel to the stem, thus provid-ing a clue to the correct response.**
10. **A key word becomes a "clue" when used in both the stem and the correct response.**

Physical Conditions

The physical conditions of the room where the test is ad-ministered are the responsibility of the teacher. How an individual feels during a test situation is affected by physical comforts, and in turn the validity of the test score is affected. The physical environment should be

[4] Charles D. Hopkins and Richard L. Antes, *Classroom Measure-ment and Evaluation* (Itasca, Ill.: F. E. Peacock Publishers, Inc., 1978) pp. 122-43.

made as comfortable as possible in order that all students have an equal opportunity to demonstrate their true achievement levels.

Teachers are well advised to provide a well-lighted, well-ventilated room which is free from noise and other distractions. There is some variation in personal desires of students regarding aspects of the physical conditions of the environment which may make it difficult to please all students; however, the teacher who is sensitive to the importance of the physical environment can provide an atmosphere conducive to optimum performance by most of the students. Since a few students may be overly sensitive to physical conditions, every effort should be made to provide optimal conditions for each test session.

ACCLIMATIZATION

Some students have a difficult time becoming accustomed to a new climate or different environment even when the size of classrooms within a building is the same. Different wall colors or materials on bulletin boards or another teacher's desk distract some students. A student feels comfortable in a familiar place and at a desk where the height of the chair and writing surface are familiar. Even when the same seat is moved to a different classroom, some students have a feeling that something has changed and it takes time for an adjustment to be made. For these reasons testing should, if at all possible, be carried out in the regular classroom where the class meets.

The "my seat" and "our classroom" has a psychological affect on some students and may determine how comfortable they feel even when a test or examination is not being administered. General adaptation to a new classroom or new surroundings has a differing effect upon student performance based on the uniqueness of each individual. For this reason students should be given a test in familiar surroundings unless other overriding factors require that the test be given someplace else.

NOISE

High noise levels during testing may result in lower test scores. Although the teacher may not have complete control of the noise level, certain arrangements may be made to lessen possible effects from noise. The season of the year and weather can affect the level and concentration of noise to particular physical locations. During inclement weather there may be more noise and distractions than usual coming from hallways and activity rooms in the school and may be disturbing to a test taker even when the classroom door is closed. Noise from students talking while they are involved in outdoor activities close to the building may be similarly distracting. Usually the area for student activity both in the building and outdoors will be limited to specified areas somewhat away from classrooms, but in some situations it may be necessary for the teacher to seek refuge with the class in some other room in the building.

Noise from recess, lunch period, band practice, and activities of other classes outside the testing room can sometimes be avoided by choosing a time when disturbing activities are unlikely. Teachers who meet classes on a schedule of modules or class periods may be limited in selection of an ideal time of day, but they should give consideration to the day of the week since some days of the week offer better conditions than others. A sign on the classroom door indicating that testing is in progress will help avoid noise and distraction from interruptions by others in the building.

The teacher must keep in mind that students have different tolerance levels for noise and other distractions. Very young children who have short attention spans can be expected to be bothered more by noise than older children who have longer attention spans. Less mature students at any age are more likely to be easily distracted than those who are grown up. To meet all students' needs in this matter requires that the teacher supply the most serene atmosphere that can be arranged.

LIGHTING

Hopefully most school classrooms will be adequately lighted even on a dreary day. The teacher can not do much to control illumination except by moving to a room with better lighting. Seasonal changes may affect the amount of light during daylight hours, and changing rooms with another teacher may be possible to provide a room with the best illumination.

If acceptable lighting conditions can not be arranged, it may be necessary to schedule a test with a "bad weather option," meaning that if it is dark and gloomy, the test will be given on an alternative test date. A teacher having a class for more than one period of the day may change the time of the day the test is given to improve the lighting conditions by taking advantage of natural light.

HEATING AND VENTILATION

The temperature of the classroom is one of the most important factors which effect the teaching-learning situation and the efficiency of students. In many classrooms the heating and ventilation of the room is set to please the teacher rather than to satisfy the majority of the students. Consideration should be given to the average temperature best for the largest number of students. When students are subjected to warmth above or coldness below recommended ranges, their efficiency is decreased. Students in kindergarten and the primary grades should be in an environment which is 65° to 68° Farenheit or 18° to 20° Celsius at shoulder height, while students in the intermediate, junior high, and senior high school grades are most efficient when 68° to 70° Fahrenheit or 20° to 21° Celsius is maintained at shoulder height.[5] Maintaining the recommended temperature may mean that some teachers will need to wear a sweater or jacket to be comfortable since s/he may feel uncomfortable at 65° Fahrenheit or 18° Celsius.

Ventilation is important to the test room since this is the primary means of controlling the temperature and humidity of the room. Also the refreshing effect of gently moving air is beneficial to all students but especially to those who feel anxious about the test session.

Other Considerations

Other factors of administration in addition to psychological and physical conditions influence the validity of the test. These considerations may overlap with the first two mentioned, but for basis of discussion they are presented at this juncture.

THE ADMINISTRATOR

The role of the teacher as test administrator is that of communicating to the students what they are to do and the conditions for doing it. For the first testing session students will need to be guided for all aspects of taking the test. After one or more administrations of tests the teacher may decide that students understand procedures so long as s/he does not change the ground rules for test taking.

If a different type of testing session requires different procedures, the changes and a review of how to function need to be given to the students. For example, if the students have taken several tests using selection-type items but this test is an essay-type test, the teacher is obliged to review how students should attack this different type of test item.

Since teachers know their own students' strengths and weaknesses, they have an opportunity to gear the administration to the level of the students in general but more importantly to individual stu-

---

[5] Basil Castaldi, *Creative Planning of Educational Facilities* (Chicago, Ill.: Rand McNally and Company, 1969), p. 213.

dents who may for one reason or another have difficulty in a test session. When deciding how much explanation to give for the test, the teacher would do better to err on the side of overexplanation rather than under-explanation. This way the student is not placed in a position of proceeding without full understanding of how to carry on with taking the test. Of course, administration of a standardized test must follow exactly the authors' instructions given in the test manual, as pointed out in a following section of this chapter.

A short statement about how the test results can aid learning is probably in order for students who are old enough to understand how testing can help them learn. The teacher's presentation should be especially pointed toward being a warm likable person so that proper rapport can be established for a testing session. Any obvious feelings of discomfort within specific students should be attended to during the test session. The teacher should also be available to explain any task which seems unclear to the student, but help must stop before it could possibly aid in selecting a correct response or give direction to an essay response. A good rule to set for the class would be to have the teacher available to help clarify tasks but not to help get right answers.

FREQUENCY AND TIME

Based upon the age of the students and the subject-matter content, the teacher must make a decision about the frequency of testing as well as the time of day for testing. Since tests motivate students to study as well as provide information concerning their learning, rather frequent testing may be necessary. A teacher may wish to administer a short quiz weekly, bi-weekly, or at some other meaningful interval of time. Longer tests and examinations should be planned and administered at appropriate times if they are needed.

Periodic testing permits the teacher to review instructional effectiveness and to reteach material that students have not comprehended satisfactorily. These tests also give students frequent information about how well they are doing in the class. Criterion-referenced tests are likely to be administered much more frequently than norm-referenced tests.

For individualized instruction, the tests are closely integrated into the teaching sequence and may even lose the identity of a test since the feedback loop into further instruction may replace marks or scores for the test session. Other individual programs, especially computer programs, include a score along with progress checks. For this reason the administration of tests for criterion-referenced measurement will take on different characteristics from norm-referenced tests.

In the elementary school, particularly at the primary level, quizzes may be given daily. The manner in which worksheets are employed in elementary classrooms may be interpreted by students as administration of quizzes or short tests. Teachers usually view this kind of in-class work more as a learning experience or as an opportunity to receive information about how well students individually and collectively have grasped important concepts and developed needed skills. When students are involved in learning which requires sequencing of skills, the need for feedback is especially great. Testing (quizzes and worksheets) thus becomes an integral part of the teaching-learning process. Recitation is also a part of the program and could be viewed as an oral testing. Whether or not elementary school teachers have taken time to reflect upon these activities as testing or instruction, the fact remains that the activities produce much the same results for students as actual test situations and many times worksheets and recitations are considered by the students to be tests.

Elementary school students are also exposed to six-weeks tests, unit tests, or tests given in some similar time span. In the late fifth or early sixth grade classroom, some teacher-made tests are oriented to six- or eight-week periods or to a unit of study rather than daily quizzes. These are employed to determine how well each student and the class as a whole have progressed and are achieving. Criterion referencing at these levels, even into adult learning, will continue with more frequent testing since progression is closely monitored by frequent administration of tests. Relatively few teachers at the elementary level administer half-year or yearly teacher-made examinations; however, classroom teachers do assist in the administration of comprehensive standardized achievement tests as scheduled.

The administration of tests in junior and senior high school is traditionally tied to marking or grading periods; however, many teachers successfully use testing plans based on different philosophies and on the nature of the subject matter that they teach. The opinions of teachers concerning frequency as well as usefulness of testing varies widely, and the number of tests administered is sometimes based on how much time is available for test preparation and administration and the amount of work required to construct, administer, and score the test and to interpret student progress. One would probably find a positive relationship between teacher understanding of how test information contributes to the instructional program and teacher attitude toward the importance of testing.

Decisions about the frequency of testing should be based on how often the teacher needs written feedback. With this consideration the teacher would probably test and make other observations at relatively frequent intervals and integrate the results that emanate from these under-takings into ongoing classroom activities.

The time when a teacher meets a specific class will deter-mine the time of day when the test can be given. Teachers who have the same students all day or for more than one class period have some flexibility in choosing the time for testing. The number of test items included and the amount of time needed for completion of the test may provide some restriction as to when the test may be administered. When the teacher is able to choose the time of the test, s/he should choose the mid-morning of a middle-of-the-week day. This is the best time, whereas just after lunch and the first thing in the morning are least appropriate in regard to student physiological functioning. The day of a major sporting event (basketball, football, etc.) or special assembly should be avoided for testing because the students' attention may be on something other than the test per se.

A generous amount of time should be provided so that nearly all students have an opportunity to respond to all of the test items. The age and ability level of students, the type of test items, and the complexity of the subject-matter content must be considered in judging the amount of time to be allotted to the test session. It is generally agreed that when items are written for the level of the student being tested, the average student should be able to respond to two true-false, one multiple-choice, or one short-answer item per minute. The time neces-sary to respond to essay items varies with the complexity of the subject content, the way the item is presented, and the depth of the response to be given. Generally, as reading skills increase, the amount of time required for responding becomes less a problem for students. The experienced teacher will be able to base the time required to respond to items on student capabilities.

MECHANICS

Preparation for actual test administration requires attention to details which are significant for carrying through what has been planned and to maximize the effects of work involved in item writing and development of a valid test. The teacher must see that one copy of the test is available for each student and is distributed at the time of the test. If separate answer sheets are used, they must be distributed at the beginning of the test session or attached to the test itself.

Distribution of material according to a plan at the start of a test session is important since time is at a premium. Oral directions and example items which may be presented should not consume valuable student response time; however, the teacher must be sure that all students understand what to do. When time is devoted to the mechanics of the test situation in class the day before a test, the test session itself runs smoother. The amount of preparation necessary on the day prior to the test depends upon the age level and general makeup of the group to be tested. Most students react favorably to a "prep" session in the class; when this is done, only a quick review is needed immediately preceding the test administration. A teacher should keep in mind that the first test session with a new group of students sets the tone for future testing and extreme care must be given to the preliminary considerations because the first test will set the stage for future test sessions with the same students.

The role of the teacher during testing is to act as proctor, to answer student questions, and to help students keep track of time. It is convenient for the teacher to have an extra supply of blank paper, pencils, and other materials on hand. In the event there is call for them, there will be no long time delay while they are obtained. If the teacher does not wear a watch, a clock or other time piece is essential, and the teacher should keep an up-date of the remaining test time on the chalkboard. Special seating arrangements, when different from everyday seating, can be handled prior to the test session, thus avoiding confusion at the beginning of the test period and eliminating use of test time to change seats.

CHEATING

Cheating on tests may be created by the stress or pressure placed upon a student by the parents, but it is more likely to be a product of lack of preparation and little study on the part of the student. The most common techniques of cheating include glancing at someone's paper, crib notes, and signals worked out between students for true-false and multiple-choice items. Cheating is dishonest, it should not be tolerated, and students should be informed that cheating will result in failure of the test and that repeated cheating means failure of the course. Careful proctoring is the most effective way to control cheating. The proctor's role is to make sure that each student has an opportunity to demonstrate his/her level of true achievement and that students are doing their own work. Administrative procedures may be taken to help deter cheating and support the proctor role. For example, the seating can be arranged so that students occupy alternative seats. Two forms of the test with the same items arranged in different order (scrambled) may be used. This technique is particularly helpful when seating arrangements are not flexible and do not allow alternate seats to be used. There is probably no way to curb all cheating entirely, but a good proctor can keep the occurrences of cheating on a test at a minimum.

Administering a Standardized Test

Administration of standardized tests is much the same as administration of teacher-made tests except that the testing sessions are controlled by more rigid adherence to the directions for administration given in the test manual. The mechanics of administration are important for determining the **reliability** and validity of the test scores, since established **norms** are based on the precision of test administration according to procedures given in the manual.

Because the results of standardized tests are compared to prepared norms, the directions for administration must be adhered to explicitly, and the test must be given under the same conditions as those used for the **norm group.** For example, if the directions specify twenty-two minutes for completing a subtest or section of the test, the administrator should keep track of the time on a stopwatch to insure that only twenty-two minutes are taken. A few seconds more or less alters a condition for testing and provides a situation which is not comparable to the way the test was designed and can affect the comparison of current students' raw scores with the norm-group scores.

The psychological considerations and physical conditions mentioned earlier in this chapter apply to the administration of a standardized test as well as the teacher-made test. The role of the classroom teacher can be that of the test administrator, although there may be situations when an outside person administers the test and the teacher assists in duties of mechanics and serves as a proctor. At other times teachers may not be allowed to participate in administration of a standardized test. The person administering the test should take time to discuss with students why the test is being given and how the test results will be used to benefit each student. The test administrator is responsible for seeing that all students have an adequate supply of sharpened pencils, quiet conditions free from interruptions, and a natural classroom situation and that students understand what they are to do in the testing session, that the proper amount of time is given, and that other details are taken care of.

TEACHER ADMINISTERS

Standardized achievement tests can be administered by any conscientious teacher. The advantage of the teacher administering the test is that a natural classroom setting is maintained since the students have had daily contacts and interactions with their teacher. Another advantage is that the teacher becomes familiar with the testing, particularly the content which the test covers. The teacher should interpret the meaning of the test scores with students after the tests have been scored.

Teachers may be assigned the responsibility of scoring the test answer sheets if they are not scored by an aide or by machine.

When preparing to administer the test, the teacher should become familiar with the contents of the manual, practice reading the directions aloud several times, and actually take the test. When other teachers are involved in administration of the test in their classrooms, teachers have an opportunity to get together to practice administration of the test using each other as subjects. If this arrangement is not possible, the teacher should administer the test to someone who will not be taking the test in school as practice experience for administration of the test. It is essential that each teacher spend the necessary time to become familiar with the entire test and administration procedures prior to actual administration in order to avoid anything in the classroom procedures that would differ from the norm-group conditions.

Since students may have taken tests with the teacher prior to administration of the standardized test, it is important for the teacher to explain that his/her role during the standardized test session is that of an impartial examiner. This means that any assistance given to the student must be permitted by the instructions in the examiner's manual. Otherwise, no assistance can be given. This is most likely a different situation from the normal classroom testing situation where the teacher may provide help in assigning tasks and giving a certain amount of guidance to students.

During testing, the teacher must accurately time the test and move around the room quietly, noting any unusual behavior or occurrences that may influence a student's score. For example, the teacher may interpret a student's behavior as an indication that the student is not trying or doing his/her best; a note made concerning this situation can be helpful when interpreting the results of this student's performance. Supervision during testing is necessary to make sure that students are correctly completing the test and recording their responses properly.

When an outside administrator gives the test, the teacher's role usually is that of being a supervisor/proctor. Whenever the size of the group being administered a test is over twenty-five students, an additional proctor is usually recommended. If the group is smaller, the teacher still can serve as a proctor for even smaller classes. Since the student-teacher relationship has already been established, the students may feel more comfortable if the teacher is there during the test session.

OUTSIDE PERSON ADMINISTERS

When a school psychometrist, school counselor, or some other person administers a standardized test, the teacher may be informed that s/he is excused to do something else during the actual testing. When an outside person administers the test, this individual has probably had extensive experience in test administration and will follow the test directions explicitly without the need for a preparation or review session. When the test is being administered to older students, there is probably no need for the teacher to be present during the test sessions if the group of students taking the test is small, but for younger students the teacher should request that s/he be permitted to assist in the supervision of the testing if it does not violate policy or test manual instructions. For younger students "their teacher's" presence can be important to the psychological atmosphere.

  This type of situation can be a learning experience for the teacher who has never administered a standardized test. Attention should be given to the test administrator's demeanor during the testing. It may be that one reason for the outside person administering the test is to provide the teacher with a situation where s/he would have the opportunity to observe and learn.

2 Scoring

In the test-planning stage the teacher decides upon the scoring procedures appropriate for the types of items to be included in a test. Ease of scoring is one factor taken into consideration when deciding on which types of items to use in the test. After the types of items to be used have been selected, questions about scoring which must be dealt with are: (1) What is the best way to organize the scoring so that it will be accurate, easy, and allow for quick return of the papers? (2) How much time will be needed to score the test papers? and (3) Who will be able to provide scoring assistance?

The ideal responses to questions raised about scoring depend on additional practical concerns about the age, ability level, and test-taking experience of the students as well as the types of items included on the test. Consideration must first be given to selection of the best situation possible for students to record responses and second the convenience to the teacher in scoring responses. Generally, early elementary students should record their responses on the test page or booklet in order to eliminate recording errors. An item skipped or one or more responses recorded out of order are likely to be difficulties experienced by very young students who are asked to record responses on a separate answer sheet. Errors by students of this age level may be contributed to by one or a combination of factors such as immaturity in cognitive development, eye development, coordination, lack of organizational capability, and inexperience in test situations. Having students record responses on the test page or sheet facilitates class discussion of the test with students since the responses are with the items. Going over the test should help students learn from their incorrect choices which, in turn, supports the instructional program. The convenience an answer sheet provides for the teacher is forgone to meet the more pressing need of the student.

At approximately the third- or fourth-grade level and up, students should be able to record responses on a separate **answer sheet** when sample items with clear and concise directions for recording are provided. Errors in recording responses occur from time to time at any grade level, although less experienced students are more apt to be frustrated and confused when recording responses. When an error which affects a series of items occurs, the teacher should take this into consideration and make an adjustment in the score of the paper. Since tests should measure achievement and not accuracy in recording responses, it is best to keep the procedure of recording responses as simple as possible, as well as suitable for students being tested.

Separate response sheets provide for more accurate and reliable scoring since all answers are recorded on one page and one type of scoring **key** can be used, which helps eliminate scoring errors. Separate response sheets should be used when students have had the maturity and experience to use them without negatively affecting the validity of the test scores.

The discussion in this chapter is devoted to general considerations of scoring, actual approaches to scoring all types of items, and the scoring of standardized tests. Scoring errors can occur with high frequency, and reduction of those errors depends on careful consideration of all aspects of the recording and scoring of responses for selection-type items and the reading and assessing of student responses to supply-type items.

Importance of Scoring

Accuracy in scoring is important because it is one of the conditions which affects the reliability of a test. The reliability of a classroom test is usually determined by using a correlation formula to compare each student's score for the odd-numbered items with the even-numbered items. The reliability of the test is determined by the ratio of the variance of the **true scores** and the variance of the obtained scores. When scoring errors occur, the obtained scores are affected, thus reducing the estimate of the test's reliability. Scoring procedures for selection-type items are objective and reduction of reliability of tests with objective items because of scoring is negligible. The subjectivity associated with scoring written responses may reduce reliability measures considerably.

Scoring of selection-type test items (true-false, multiple-choice, matching, and classification) is expected to be very accurate if proper scoring procedures are established when the test is planned and after it is given. Objectivity in scoring is characteristic of selection-type items since alternatives from which the student may choose are provided and responses are checked against a key. If more than one person were asked to score selection-type items, the total score obtained on any paper scored would always be the same unless a clerical error occurs; therefore, given good scoring procedures, the scoring of selection-type items should affect neither the reliability nor the validity of the test.

Scoring supply-type items (completion, short answer, and essay), because of the nature of the items, makes reliability of scoring an earnest concern. Scorer reliability refers to the agreement of scores for two or more readers, or independent readings by one reader, the higher the scorer reliability the higher the correlation coefficient.[1] The reliability coefficient is more likely to be low when there is extensive subjectivity in scoring. The subjectivity can result in scoring error which has the effect of lowering reliability coefficients. When scoring is inconsistent, the difference between what the test paper deserves and what it receives will be increased. As chance errors are reduced, the reliability coefficient will be greater. Special attention must be given to assure a high level of consistency in scoring supply-type items, especially essay items.

The accuracy of scoring affects the reliability of the test and, in turn, the validity of the test. A test is valid to the degree it accurately measures what it was constructed to measure. If a classroom test is to generate valid scores, its scores must be highly reliable, and accurate scoring contributes much to that reliability component of test validity.

General Considerations

Test-scoring procedures must generate accurate scores as quickly as possible so that test papers and test results can be returned promptly to students. In addition, the scorer should indicate which items have been responded to incorrectly and clearly mark correct responses for missed items for student reference. This procedure assists the students when reviewing items and avoids wasting class time when the teacher must read the correct responses one-by-one as students mark correct answers for those they missed.

When a teacher employs true-false or multiple-choice items, s/he should compute an **item analysis.** The analysis provides an examination of student general performance for each item on a test by

---

[1] For further discussion of the reliability coefficient, see Charles D. Hopkins and Richard L. Antes, *Classroom Measurement and Evaluation* (Itasca, Ill.: F. E. Peacock Publishers, Inc., 1978), pp. 261-91.

applying mathematical techniques to assess two characteristics of true-false and multiple-choice items—**difficulty** and **discrimination.** For all other types of items, as well as true-false and multiple-choice, if the teacher does not use a formal item analysis, s/he should compile a record/tabulation of student errors in order to answer questions such as the following: What is the ratio of the high-scoring to low-scoring students who missed specific items? Of the total number of students in the class what percentage responded correctly to specific items? Did students understand the subject matter content? Based on responses to test items, was the class presentation adequate in the subject-matter content? Did the test items communicate clearly to students in regard to what was being tested by the items? These questions, and possibly others, may be answered more accurately if a record of student responses is made and studied.

Controversy exists over whether students learn from scoring their classmate's test papers after taking a test. Some teachers feel that the exchange of papers for scoring immediately after the test is a learning experience. Generally, educators find that students are so concerned with how they responded to each item that they have a difficult, if not impossible, time being truly attentive to scoring another classmate's paper. Their attention is directed to recalling how they responded and whether the response was correct or incorrect rather than the task at hand—scoring a classmate's paper. In-class scoring usually leads to inaccuracy in scoring, and the papers must be rescored by the teacher or an aide after the original session, thus consuming additional time. It is the authors' opinion that class time can be utilized for more important activities than the clerical task of scoring test papers.

Test papers should be quickly scored and promptly returned to students. Before administering a test, the teacher should plan for quick turnaround of the test results to avoid the overanxiousness of students and to allow reteaching material before going on to something else. The more immediate the feedback, the more effectively it will support learning. This is of extreme importance when topics are sequential and attainment of prerequisite skills is necessary before additional subject matter can be introduced.

A teacher may find after beginning to score a group of papers that the scoring can be completed more efficiently by altering the original scoring scheme. Good testing and previous scoring experience provide the teacher with ideas for adaptations which make the scoring process better. Flexibility in making adjustments in the scoring process should occur whenever necessary to make the scoring less time consuming and more efficient for the scorer.

Scoring Selection-Type Items

Selection-type items (true-false, multiple-choice, matching, and classification) require the student to select from the alternatives provided. The method of scoring is determined by the way students were asked to record their responses. Three methods of scoring selection-type items are: hand-scoring, self-scoring, and machine-scoring. Each of these has advantages and limitations depending on such factors as the time, cost, and personnel available to assist in scoring.

A moderate amount of time is required to hand-score a test of any length, although the time does not have to be the teacher's time if a secretary, aide, or other clerical worker is available to score the test papers. Whether or not clerical help is provided for hand-scoring of tests depends on the particular situation or school policy. Generally, if assistance is needed, a secretary or some part-time employee may be available to provide scoring assistance as part of the overall responsibilities in the school office. In some situations office personnel may run scoring machines as well as carry out duplication of materials for teachers. In any case, except for the possibility of clerical errors, the number of correct responses on each paper will be the same regardless of who is scoring the paper, since judgment is not needed to compare the keyed responses with those recorded on the answer sheet.

Machine scoring can be completed quickly and accurately with limited teacher involvement if a scoring machine is available. Self-scoring answer sheets, which provide immediate feedback to students through a special way of recording responses, require that extra time be given during the testing situation for students to respond to the items since more than one response may be marked before the correct answer is selected. A limited amount of teacher time is required to total the correct responses for the final score. The teacher may ask each student to total the correct responses for a self-scoring test.

Self-scoring sheets are more expensive than either answer sheets duplicated in the school or machine-scorable sheets. The initial investment for the scoring machine may be relatively high, although it is a rather permanent piece of equipment which can provide years of service and can serve one or more school buildings. Hand-scoring is inexpensive since the answer sheets can be reproduced by spirit duplicating and mimeograph. Hand-scoring sheets are always readily available, while self-scoring, machine-scoring sheets or cards must be ordered, purchased, and kept on hand. The availability of machine scoring rests upon the budget commitments of the school and the availability of scoring machines. The three factors (time, cost, and personnel available to assist in scoring) discussed interact and are considered jointly when decisions are made concerning what type of test-scoring services are to be made available to teachers.

HAND-SCORING PROCEDURES

Hand scoring involves the checking of student's responses to objective test items by the teacher or a helper with the use of a key, stencil, or other device. When responses are recorded in the spaces provided on the test page, the scorer may develop a key by recording the correct responses on a copy of the test. Each student's paper is compared to the keyed responses, and a colored pencil is used to mark the correct response when it has not been selected. By marking a slash through an incorrect response and recording the correct response, the scorer draws the student's attention to the correct response. This procedure also helps the scorer to count the number of correct or incorrect responses and to figure each student's raw score (the number of items answered correctly). With the aid of a key the entire scoring process can be completed by someone with no knowledge of the subject content tested. Directions for using the key can be explained to a clerical worker and the complete scoring process handled with relatively few directions from the teacher. Once an individual has had the experience of scoring a set of papers, s/he can score additional sets of papers routinely.

When responses are recorded on the left-hand margin of the test itself, an accordian or fan key can be used efficiently in scoring. The accordian or fan key can be developed by folding an 8½ inch by 11 inch sheet of paper lengthwise three times, providing four columns the length of the page. The columns are two inches wide, allowing room for the keyed (correct) responses to be recorded. If the responses are recorded on the test, they are spaced on the key to correspond with the spacing of items on the test page. Figure 2.1 presents a sample accordian or fan key for scoring responses.

The key is conveniently placed along the column of responses which have been recorded in the left margin of each page. Correct responses are marked on the key for each item and compared to the responses made by the student. If the correct response is A and B is written on the paper, a slash line should be drawn through B and the correct response, A, written for feedback to the student. As discussed earlier, providing correct responses will facilitate discussion when the papers are returned to students.

Selection-type tests scored on the item page or booklet usually have more than one page. By scoring all items on the first page for all papers, second page for all papers, and so on, the scorer can save time,

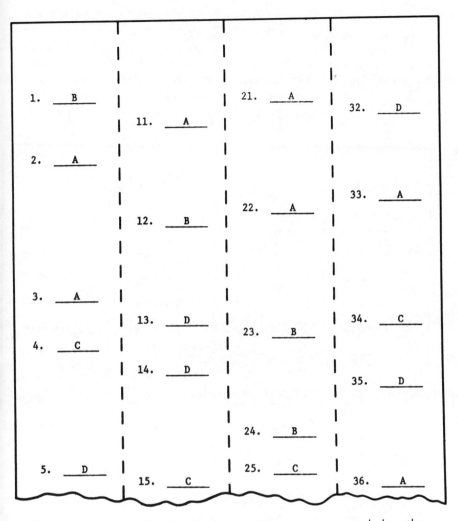

Figure 2.1 Accordian or fan key for scoring responses recorded on the test sheet.

thus making scoring efficiency higher. The speed and accuracy of scoring is facilitated by arranging papers with the same page to be scored, scoring them, and then folding the next page to be scored. When papers are hand scored, they should be double-checked by another scorer. If this is not possible, a sample of papers may be checked in their entirety. When an error is found on a page, all other papers should be checked for the same error.

When a separate response sheet is provided, equal spacing of the lines can be used, as shown in Figure 2.2. When the paper is folded along the vertical broken lines, an accordian or fan key is developed. When the paper is cut along the vertical broken lines, it is known as a strip key. Strip keys may be easier to use if they are made of cardboard or stiff paper. Hand-scoring devices can be made of materials such as paper, card stock, or transparent materials. Most classroom tests, particularly for

1. A	26. A	51. B	76. A
2. B	27. C	52. B	77. C
3. A	28. C	53. A	78. A
4. C	29. B	54. C	79. D
5. C	30. D	55. D	80. B
6. D	31. A	56. A	81. C
7. A	32. C	57. D	82. B
8. C	33. C	58. B	83. D
9. D	34. A	59. C	84. A
10. A	35. D	60. D	85. C
11. B	36. B	61. C	86. D
12. C	37. C	62. A	87. A
13. A	38. D	63. B	88. D
14. D	39. B	64. C	89. A
15. C	40. A	65. D	90. D
	41.	6	C

Figure 2.2 Accordian or fan key for scoring responses recorded on a separate answer sheet.

the elementary grades, are scored by one of the keys presented unless they are very long tests.

The response sheet in Figure 2.3 requires the student to mark a response by circling and shading the circled letter of the selected alternative or to mark an X through the letter chosen. This type of response sheet may be scored with a stencil as shown in Figure 2.4 or with an accordian, fan, or strip key. The black dots in Figure 2.4 represent holes which have been punched in heavy paper or card stock. The stencil is placed over the answer sheet, and holes where nothing appears are marked in red, which provides for a count of the items missed and marks the correct response for student inspection. Scanning the response sheet prior to scoring permits items with more than one response to be marked as incorrect by marking in red across all alternatives.

Earlier it was mentioned that most selection-type classroom tests may be scored by one of the scoring keys presented unless they

RESPONSE SHEET

Name _____

DIRECTIONS: After choosing the best response mark your choice by shading the letter which represents your choice.

Example: A B Ⓒ D

1.	A B C D	26.	A B C D	51.	A B C D	76.	A B C D
2.	A B C D	27.	A B C D	52.	A B C D	77.	A B C D
3.	A B C D	28.	A B C D	53.	A B C D	78.	A B C D
4.	A B C D	29.	A B C D	54.	A B C D	79.	A B C D
5.	A B C D	30.	A B C D	55.	A B C D	80.	A B C D
6.	A B C D	31.	A B C D	56.	A B C D	81.	A B C D
7.	A B C D	32.	A B C D	57.	A B C D	82.	A B C D
8.	A B C D	33.	A B C D	58.	A B C D	83.	A B C D

Figure 2.3 Separate response sheet.

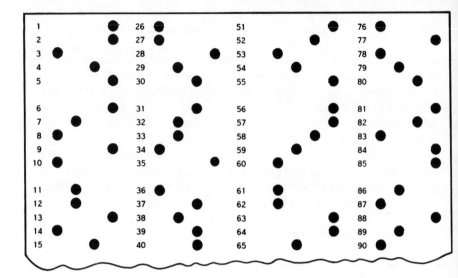

Figure 2.4 Punched scoring key.

are very long tests. If a test is very long and/or the teacher has a large number of papers to score, an overprinting process may be utilized. This process consists of development of a key on a stencil or spirit master. The key stencil is run on a duplicating machine over the completed student-response sheets, and incongruent responses are counted. Alignment can be checked by running a few blank trial response sheets through the duplicating machine prior to placing student responses into the machine to make sure alignment is correct.

SELF-SCORING PROCEDURES

Self-scoring answer sheets provide a method of marking responses to objective test items in such a way that the test taker knows immediately whether the response is correct or incorrect. These commercially available recording devices score the test for the student as s/he selects options to items after the teacher has keyed the correct response for each item to the prekeyed response on the self-scoring sheet. Several different variations of the self-scoring devices are available through different companies. In one type of self-scoring device an erasure uncovers a letter which the student can interpret as a correct or incorrect response according to a code. Another type of self-scoring response sheet employs a latent image printed in invisible ink which is made visible when a light coating from a chemical marker pen "develops" the ink, and the mark is interpreted as a correct or incorrect response according to a code.

The directions for the response sheet or card tell the student to indicate his/her chosen response by erasing the block or marking the appropriate space with the chemical marker. An erasure or chemical mark reveals whether or not the student has chosen the prekeyed correct response. With the use of the self-scoring sheet, the student may continue to mark responses until the correct one appears. Self-scoring devices permit a student to have from one to five tries, depending upon the self-scoring sheet used and the directions supplied by the teacher. In cases where the student has second, third, or fourth tries to obtain the correct answer, a point assignment may be employed. The following schemes provide examples of point systems for four- and five-choice devices.

Correct response upon	4-choice device; points assigned	5-choice device; points assigned
1st erasure	3	4
2nd erasure	2	3
3rd erasure	1	2
4th erasure	0	1
5th erasure		0

The student uses this table to add the points in each column and inserts the total points at the top of the response card or sheet. The teacher checks the response sheet after the test session.

Ideally, a self-scoring device counters the point of view that no learning takes place during testing. Through immediate feedback the student is reinforced in learning when selecting the correct response. When more than one attempt at the correct response is required, the student, upon selecting the correct response, learns the correct idea or concept and receives immediate feedback. This approach also supports the suggestion that it is best to correct errors in previous learning prior to moving on to new learning experiences.

In reality, immediate feedback affects students differently. For example, a student who has a high self-concept and achieves at a moderate to high level is least likely to be hampered in performance when confronted with the situation of making two, three or four choices for an item to obtain the correct response. On the other hand, a student with a low self-concept who misses one or two items early in the test may become emotionally frustrated and his/her ability to perform to his/her real level of performance during the remainder of the test might be inhibited. In this situation the student does not learn from errors and probably is unable to think clearly when selecting responses to subsequent items.

The logical conclusion to be drawn about whether to use self-scoring answer sheets or some other type depends on the composition of the class and the individual needs of the learners. If a student is frustrated by the self-scoring answer sheet and if attention from the teacher cannot overcome this difficulty, then another scoring method should be used with this student.

MACHINE-SCORING PROCEDURES

Machine scoring answer sheets for true-false and multiple-choice tests is becoming more popular although the cost of a scoring machine has limited their availability for scoring classroom achievement tests. Small scoring machines are more likely to be utilized in moderate to large school systems. They appear occasionally in some smaller more progressive schools or at a school where one or more members of the faculty have convinced the administration of the value of having a scoring machine. In some instances, civic organizations and other groups may have been persuaded to purchase a scoring machine for a school or school system.

Scoring by machine today is most likely to utilize the optical scanning system, using the transmitted light principle or the reflected-light principle. These mark-scan machines detect/read marks on an answer sheet or card. Figure 2.5 illustrates an answer sheet on which the alternative chosen is indicated by using a soft lead pencil to mark by blackening (shading in) small ovals that correspond to the choices for all items. General purpose response sheets are designed for multiple-choice and true-false items. The first two answer spaces are utilized for true-false items, the first space for true and the second space for false. Four- or five-choice multiple-choice items utilize the 1/A, 2/B, 3/C, 4/D, or 5/E spaces available.

By use of a phototransistor or photoelectric "eye" the scanner reads a complete row across the answer sheet at once and relays the right and/or wrong responses electronically for counting of the total number right. Scoring machines are available that scan answer sheets at the rate of 100 per minute and count the number of right responses at the rate of 10,000 per second.

Optical scanning equipment can be connected to a computer which enables generation of a variety of information. For example, columns can be printed which list the names, the number of correct responses, the number of incorrect responses, and the standard score for each student. The mean and standard deviation in raw score units and

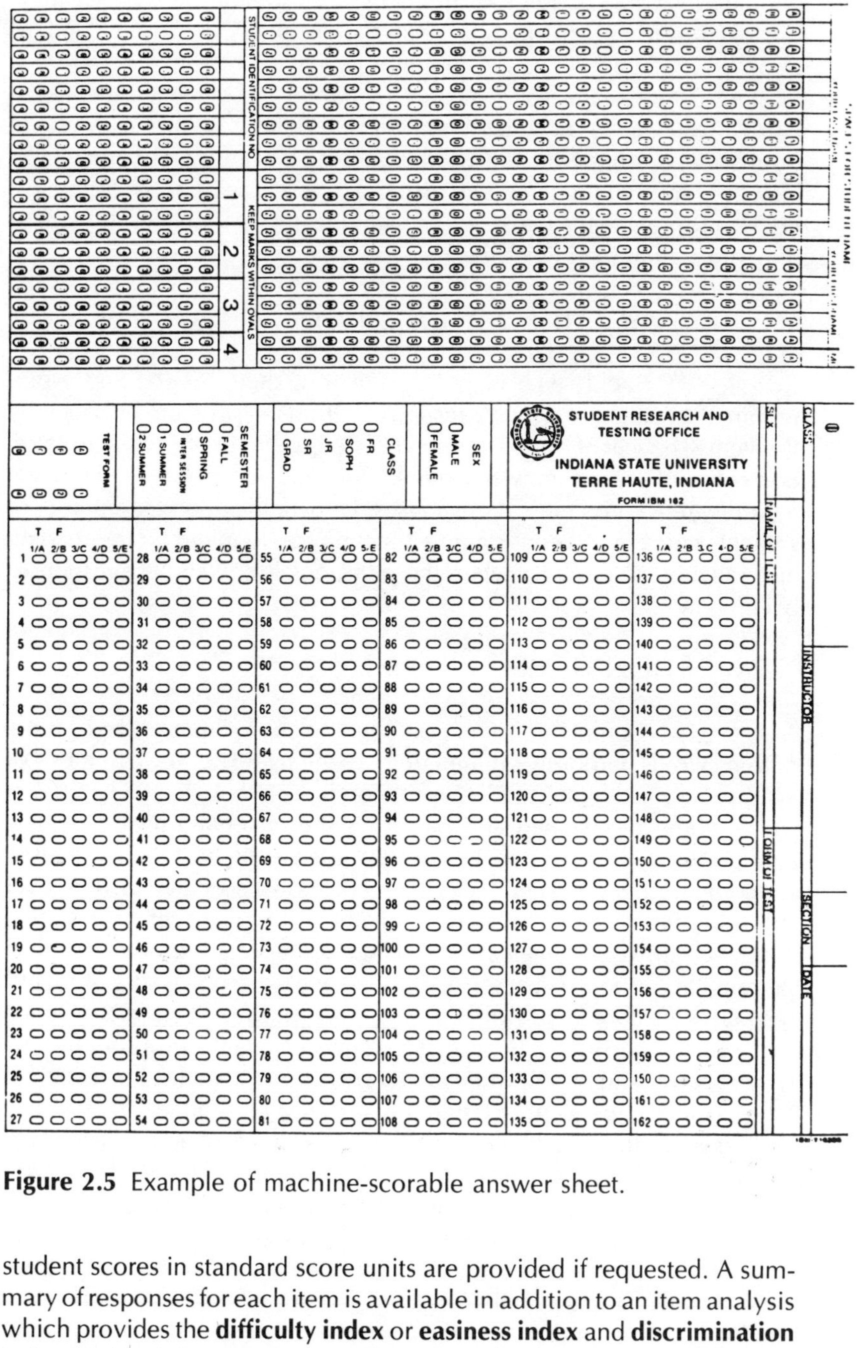

Figure 2.5 Example of machine-scorable answer sheet.

student scores in standard score units are provided if requested. A summary of responses for each item is available in addition to an item analysis which provides the **difficulty index** or **easiness index** and **discrimination index.** Other information about the test and other summary statistical data are available as follows: frequency distribution, percentile table, histogram, answer distribution analysis, skewness, kurtosis, standard error, and reliability. The additional information can be entered on a master printout for the teacher's use. A separate printout that provides the correct response for each item and each student's response is available from some scoring services. Machine scoring is accurate and efficient as well as helpful in judging the worth of the test. The analysis of the test items may provide the teacher with valuable information for future planning of teaching and learning.

Scoring Supply-Type Items

Supply-type items (completion, short answer, and essay) require the student to create a response within the structure provided by the item. The teacher or someone knowledgeable in the subject-matter content must score supply-type items since judgments have to be made regarding the correctness of responses. Depending upon the number of students being tested considerable time may be required for the reading and judging, particularly when the decisions for essay item responses become tedious.

COMPLETION ITEMS

Completion items ask the student to supply one or more missing words purposely omitted from a sentence. The word, number, or symbol supplied by the student must complete a thought and be correct in the context presented and based on the material which has been studied. A cutout or window key, as illustrated in Figure 2.6, may be used in scoring responses when they are recorded in a scattered fashion over the test page. The stencil may be made of heavy paper or a similar substance in which holes are cut. Placing the stencil on the test page permits the response spaces to show through the holes. The students' responses are compared with the correct responses written on the stencil to the left or right of each window. Optional acceptable responses may be written above and/or below the cutout windows. Flexibility is required in scoring since equivalent or parallel words may be supplied by students. The response the teacher wishes to see may be keyed in the usual way although additional responses which should be counted correct may show up in scoring. Other than for the aspect of additional correct answers, the scoring procedure is very similar to scoring an objective test.

When a separate answer sheet is provided and the responses are recorded near the left-hand margin of the paper, a scoring key similar to the accordian key may be utilized in scoring. The correct

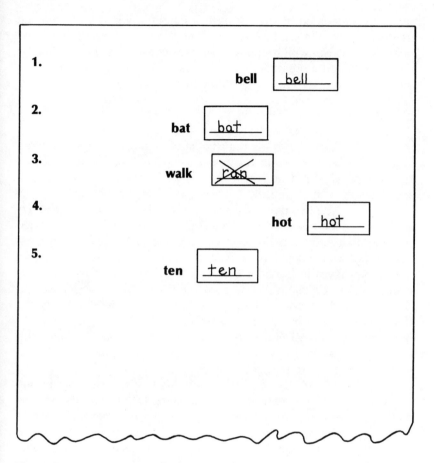

Figure 2.6 Cutout or window scoring key.

word(s) are written on the key instead of the letter, number, or symbol employed with selection items. The total number of correct responses are counted and recorded on each student paper.

SHORT-ANSWER ITEMS

Short-answer items ask the student to respond with more than one word but not a complete sentence or statement. The short-answer format presents a direct question rather than a statement with a part omitted. It may require the same type of response as a completion item and may be scored in the same manner as the completion item. When the short-answer response which is somewhat less than a complete sentence is recorded on the test page, a cutout or window key may be used in scoring. For separate answer sheets the key should provide the possible responses which would be counted correct. The teacher's judgment is required more often in scoring the short-answer item than it is with the more objective completion item.

ESSAY ITEMS

Essay items ask the student to organize a response into a complete thought in one or more written sentences. The freedom allowed by this type of item generates responses which must be assessed by a scorer who is knowledgeable in the subject-matter content.

The two types of essay items available for use by teachers are the extended-response and the limited-response item. The extended response has no definite limits to restrict the student response (the possible response coverage is open ended) while the limited response asks a question or gives instructions that limit the area to be covered in the response (the possible response coverage is well fenced-in for the students). Since the scope of the expected answer has definite limits, the limited-response essay item is appropriate for use in classroom achievement tests and the extended-response essay item is more suitable for English or other language arts classes where development of skills of written expression is an objective.

Scoring of the limited-response essay item may be approached from the analytical or global method. Both of these scoring methods attempt to combat the main criticism that judgment of responses enters heavily into scoring of essay tests thus reducing the reliability of the resulting measures. The problem of scoring essay items with high reader realiability lies in the subjectivity associated with scorer judgments. Consistency in essay scoring is reduced as different raters assign different marks to the same essay response. In addition, even a single rater tends to assign different scores to the same essay response on different occasions. The greater the freedom of response, the greater the differences. As students are allowed to write more varied answers, the reader must be more flexible; and the more flexibility, the greater the likelihood of lessened reliability in the measures.

The reliability of scoring can be increased by giving attention to the details of item construction. Essay items should be phrased and framed to elicit the response desired. Explicit directions and careful wording of the question on establishment of the **task** to be performed help the student to respond. An outline of the expected response noting important points should be written by the scorer. Careful attention to the characteristics and major points provide scoring guidelines when the amount of credit to be given each point is specified. Identifying the major points and characteristics of the expected or ideal response also assists the teacher in being more explicit in stating the actual essay item. If a response is written before the test is administered, flaws may be identified and the item revised before it appears on the student test.

The decision about the most appropriate scoring method should be made prior to essay testing. Advocates of the essay examination employ one of two methods in scoring essay responses depending on which best fits the conditions. The analytical method, also referred to as the point method, attempts to provide a detailed guide to scoring by identifying crucial elements of the ideal response and weighting the relative importance of the elements. The global method, also referred to as the relative rating or holistic method, concentrates on the global ratings of the responses based on standards as determined by the overall student response to an essay item. The method chosen for evaluating essay responses may depend on the content of the subject area being examined and behaviors desired.

Analytical Method

When the teacher has chosen the analytical method of scoring, s/he should keep the following points concerning marking the responses in mind:

1. Prior to beginning the scoring process, a model response to each essay item is written.
2. The major elements to be identified are placed in outline form.
3. Point values to be assigned from the major elements of the response are determined.
4. Additional factors, if any, to be given consideration in scoring, such as organization, and integration, correctness of expression, completeness of response, and other concerns important to the teacher, are determined and the point values set down.
5. The detailed scoring guide is applied to each student's paper as the teacher attempts to identify the crucial elements of each item.
6. A point value is assigned to each response.
7. The final total score is arrived at by totaling the points assigned to each item, and this becomes the test score.

The teacher will find the analytical scoring procedure time consuming, tedious and tiresome when a large number of papers is scored by this method, but the time spent should result in highly reliable test scores.

Global Method

When the teacher chooses the global method of scoring, s/he should keep the following points concerning marking the responses in mind:

1. **In the first reading, the scorer reads the responses, developing an overall impression of the adequacy of each response.**
2. **Based on this reading, the scorer tentatively assigns each paper to a category according to the quality of the response.**
3. **The number of categories is contingent upon the desires of the scorer and the levels of discrimination needed. Usually four or five categories are used.**
4. **Reference points are established by determining a top level and lowest level of responses and fitting other categories between.**
5. **A second, more careful reading allows for a shift from the tentative category to refine the groupings.**
6. **A third reading of the papers by groups provides verification that the categorization is correct. The scorer determines whether or not the papers in each group are about the same level of accomplishment. Any paper in any group which appears to rate above or below that group can be moved accordingly.**
7. **A letter grade or numerical score is assigned to each paper according to which category it fell in.**

The global method can be used to score a large number of essay responses reliably. The main limitation is that the scoring rationale is difficult to explain to students, and the letter grade or numerical score is difficult to justify.

Considerations for Scoring Essay Responses

There is a proportional relationship between the number of papers and the amount of time and effort required for scoring essay responses. These factors influence which item type a teacher will use. Most teachers will lean toward and rely heavily on the selection-type item because of the greater ease, efficiency, and accuracy of scoring. However, the essay-type item is more useful for measuring the more complex categories of learning and for measuring in some ways not possible if selection-type items are used. When teachers choose essay items, they should keep the following points in mind:

1. Anonymous scoring of responses prevents the scorer from being influenced by the past performance of students. It is nearly impossible not to be influenced by the previous achievement of students in the evaluation of essay responses, even when a sincere attempt is made to judge the responses solely on the basis of what is written. Identification numbers, names on the reverse side of the pages, and other procedures

can help to provide anonymous scoring of papers. After scoring the papers, the teacher can match the names to the number or other code employed. In some cases the scorer may recognize handwriting, but an attempt to read and react to the responses separate from the writer are important to reduction of the effects of bias.

2. When using analytical scoring, the scorer should determine scores for all responses to item one before scoring responses to item two. The scorer should not determine scores for item three until all responses to item two have been scored, and so on. Since consistency in judgment is increased by concentrating on one item at a time, this method will increase scorer reliability. Also the effect of a student's performance on one item should not influence the score for the next item if this procedure is adhered to.

3. If deemed practical and not too expensive, the response for each item on the test can be written on a separate sheet of paper. If the answers are short, this may be impractical. If more than one answer is on the same page, the point values for each item can be recorded on a sheet to include all points for all items.

4. To avoid variation in the scorer's reaction based on time lag between scoring papers, all responses to an item should be scored in one time period. All scorers are human and may be affected by various factors from day to day even from morning to afternoon which may change reactions to items read and values assigned.

5. When scoring criteria are used in analytical scoring, the criteria are compared to the responses. The teacher thus becomes aware of his/her expectations (model response) in reference to student responses. A judgment can be made concerning how realistic the model response is and whether some adjustment is necessary after reading several responses.

6. When the mechanics of writing, spelling, quality of expression, and other factors are to be scored, they should be judged separately on a sheet of paper specifically used for this purpose. Students need to be informed, prior to testing, if factors other than content of the response will be included in the overall assessment of the response.

7. Comments and corrections written on the paper provide important feedback to the student and support learning. A record and tally of common misunderstandings or other things about which students should know as a group are helpful in planning future decisions and instruction.

8. Reader reliability can be increased through independent reading by two or more scorers. The teacher and a colleague should mark the papers independently, and their two scores should be averaged. Any wide discrepancies between scores should be reconciled.

When necessary, the teacher can record the scores on the back of each paper, laying the papers aside for a few days and then reevaluating them again and averaging the scores. This procedure causes more delay in returning the papers, which is not the optimum situation, but it is better than one reading. When a teacher gives an essay test, s/he must give each student's responses careful consideration. When the factors mentioned are taken seriously, they will increase the reliability of scoring and student morale.

Scoring Standardized Tests

Whether the teacher or an outside person administers the standardized test, the teacher may be expected to score the test when a small number of students is tested. When a large number of students is tested, the answer sheets will most likely be scored by machine either at a local or national scoring service. Most test publishers include scoring service and statistical data reporting as part of the package testing service, although some publishers may subcontract the actual scoring and data reporting service. The two important aims in scoring standardized tests are (1) completing the scoring accurately and (2) completing the task as soon as possible.

HAND-SCORING

When responses are recorded on the test booklet, the scoring often is completed by hand by each classroom teacher. Hand scoring is a routine clerical task which most teachers consider mundane and time consuming. It is possible for teachers to work together to reduce the time required for scoring as well as providing a check on the original scoring. In some instances, the teacher can solicit assistance in the scoring process from persons who volunteer or receive pay for assisting in the scoring. Whether the teacher scores the answer sheets, works with other teachers cooperatively, or receives outside clerical assistance, s/he should set aside some time for a preparation session before the answer sheets are actually scored. Someone who has had experience in scoring the particular test which was given should teach the proper procedure for scoring the test answer sheets. The manual and scoring key should be thoroughly studied and the actual scoring process demonstrated. Each individual should then be provided with a supervised experience in scoring at least one student's answer sheet. Anyone scoring tests should understand the use of scoring guides, procedures for marking and counting responses, and any other considerations which apply to the specific test to be scored. The time and effort taken in this preparation session will help reduce the errors often associated with hand-scoring procedures.

Each test should be checked through a second scoring by another individual. An alternative would be to spot-check items for scoring accuracy. The importance of accurate scoring in order to insure the reliability and validity of the test should be stressed.

When separate answer sheets are used, all the responses are on one page, which facilitates scoring. A separate answer sheet may also reduce the cost of replacing test booklets. The separate answer sheet can be scored by one of several processes, depending upon the type of answer sheet selected. A stencil scoring key supplied by the test publisher can be used. The stencil is usually made of a light cardboard or heavy paper with holes punched to correspond to the correct responses. The stencil is laid over an answer sheet and the holes where no marks occur are marked with a colored pencil and counted as incorrect responses. One caution to be kept in mind is that each answer sheet must be scanned to determine if any items have been marked with more than one response since duplicate responses are not picked-up when the stencil scoring key is placed over an answer sheet. Figure 2.4 is an example of the punched scoring key made by the teacher for his/her classroom test. The commercially produced stencil scoring key uses the same principle as a teacher-made stencil key.

For some tests a carbon answer sheet may be purchased from certain test publishers. This type of answer sheet consists of a carbon paper sealed between two answer sheets. As the student marks the responses on the top sheet, the bottom sheet is marked by the carbon paper, which is face down between the two pages. To score the answer sheet the scorer tears the pages apart, locates the number of marks in the circles or squares of the bottom sheet, counts and records the number of correct choices.

A similar type of commercially available hand-scoring sheet consists of two sealed sheets. The student pushes a stylus or pin through the response selected. When the two sheets are detached, the pinprick, if the correct choice was made, appears in the circle or square. The correct selections are counted and the number recorded. Some type of backing sheet is provided with the answer sheets to prevent the pin from contacting the student or desk top. The selection of the scoring key is usually based upon the cost and availability of the types of keys from various test publishers as well as the preference of the personnel at the school level.

MACHINE SCORING

The most error-free scoring method which also relieves teachers from the task of scoring standardized tests is machine scoring. The services of electrical or electronic machines for scoring are available from test publishers or some centralized commercial scoring company. Machine scoring by a service agency, although more accurate, may cause a delay in scoring, and it may be a few or even several weeks before the scoring results and subsequent statistical data are returned to the school.

The optical scoring equipment can translate test-score response information to computers which provide for full exploitation of the test data. Scoring services have optional programs available to convert raw scores to different types of derived scores. Printed reports of the scoring, derived scores, comparisons to national norms, development, and comparison to local norms are a few of the services that may be purchased.

Scoring machines used by test publishers and test-scoring agencies are quite expensive but are flexible and can handle scoring sheets from many different tests and different formats. Considering the amount and kinds of information that they can generate for sets of scores and for individual scores, the cost to the school system is relatively inexpensive. The principles used in developing machines for scoring large volumes of answer sheets from standardized tests have been used to develop some simpler machines for answer sheets from classroom tests and schoolwide testing. Turnaround time for scoring answer sheets can be kept to a reasonable minimum if well-organized procedures are used.

3 Whadjagit?

A test is administered to serve one or more of several purposes, but the usual reason for spending class time to conduct a testing session is to measure student achievement. A test occasionally is administered to measure another construct such as aptitude or interest, but classroom tests and standardized tests that measure achievement make up most of the tests given to students.

School-program effectiveness and student-achievement levels are important factors to be considered when making decisions about what school learning activities are working the way that they should and those which need to be altered or discontinued. Decisions which are made by and for each student also must be based on judgments which have been made from a wide information base. A substantial part of that information is generated by tests; however, consideration of other information collected by direct observation and other nontesting procedures is important to decision making.

Logic tells us that a study of the educational process must be a study of students, since they are what make the process of education work. Decisions are made at many times and for different reasons, but each one must be based on judgments made about student performance. Decision makers include school board members, parents, students, teachers, principals, superintendents, program directors, guidance personnel, diagnostic teams, and researchers. Each asks for information about student performance as individually or collectively they make educationally oriented decisions about groups of students or a student individually.

For the above reason, school board members and school administrators at all levels ask for test information with the question, "What did you get?" The administrator's "you" includes all students who fall within a well-defined geographical area, which may be as large as the nation or as small as a school district. The question is answered by looking at the test scores from a national sample of students or scores reported in a statewide, school district, or individual school testing program.

For the same reason, the classroom teacher asks, "What did you get?" The teacher's "you" includes both the students as a group and as individuals. At this level the student receives individual consideration, and evaluation of the educational process focuses more directly on individual performance while keeping in mind that each student is to a great degree a product of school experience.

After a testing session, students also want to know what other students got, but they ask the question for a different reason. The student's "Whadjagit?" asks for information from others so that s/he can find out how the score on her/his paper compares to other students' test scores. The student's "you" is singular, but it is asked of many students who also took the test. The student builds a frame of reference by using the set of scores which s/he knows. This gives a general idea about what a specific score means in terms of what the peer group did on the test, thus indicating an estimate of relative performance for that student's score.

Using Test Scores

To answer the questions "What did you get?" and "Whadjagit?" certain steps must be taken to make test scores meaningful by showing what each test score stands for. After the papers have been scored and a raw score assigned to each student's responses, the teacher must interpret what the score means. A test score in isolation means nothing, and some way of interpreting it must be used to make sense of what the student has exhibited in the particular test session. When in the classroom, the teacher provides the class with some reference system to make comparisons easier and to give the individual score meaning.

The next three chapters cover ways to interpret test scores. This chapter establishes the needs of persons who use test data gathered in the classroom and explains why students are repeatedly asked to supply data by taking tests.

ADMINISTRATOR NEEDS

"Study Shows Youths Lacking in Three Essential Writing Skills."[1] Who says this? How was this determined? Who asked the original question?

[1] "Writing Skills Lacking 'Essential Trio'" *NAEP Newsletter* (October 1977).

To answer the questions in order, first, the report came from a National Assessment of Educational Progress (NAEP) assessment of students' writing expression. Second, it was uncovered in 1974 when students all over the country were asked to write and revise their writings during testing sessions conducted in the students' classrooms. Third, the question was asked by educators, especially administrators and curriculum builders, who deal with education at the national level.

In the middle sixties, a series of events resulted in creation of an organization to assess educational progress on a national level. The first assessment was conducted in 1969 for the learning areas of science, citizenship, and writing. Using these data for baseline comparisons, later studies of the same areas can reveal general effectiveness of school programs. Figure 3.1 lists the learning areas as they were covered year by year through 1980. Information from this broad data base allows those who deal with education on the national scope opportunity to identify where changes in instructional programs are needed.

School Year   **Learning Area Assessed in Schools**

(Results reported approximately one year after data collection completed)

School Year	Learning Area Assessed in Schools
1969-70	Science, citizenship, writing
1970-71	Reading, literature
1971-72	Music, social studies
1972-73	Science (second assessment), mathematics
1973-74	Writing (second assessment), career and occupational development
1974-75	Reading (second assessment), art
1975-76	Citizenship/social studies (second assessment)
1976-77	Science (third assessment); special probe: basic life skills
1977-78	Mathematics (second assessment); special probe: consumerism
1978-79	Writing (third assessment), art and music (second assessment)
1979-80	Reading (third assessment), literature (second assessment)

Figure 3.1 NAEP's assessment schedule.

SOURCE: *(NAEP Newsletter,* August 1977)

A testing program at a state level provides data bases for a limited geographic area, but it exists for the same reason the NAEP exists. Some of the state programs have adopted many techniques used in national assessment, and many use some of the data collected in their states by the national program. School districts utilize much the same approach in their testing programs. At national, state, and local levels the administration staffs ask for information which will indicate to them how well their students, in general, did on tests. Interpretation of test scores must be made in such a way that evaluations which use test scores and other observations are valid. The final decisions require clear communication from student performances to the evaluation stage and on to the decision maker if educational programs are to be improved. The sequence is started with adequate interpretation of student scores in reply to the administrator's question of "What did you get?"

TEACHER NEEDS

Teachers are more directly related to a more limited sample of students—those with whom they deal every day. The elementary school teacher may have the same twenty to thirty students in one room for all subjects. At the other extreme, junior and senior high school teachers who teach one or two subjects may have six to eight classes a day with twenty to thirty students in each class. These teachers may have classroom contact with two hundred or more students each day. Certainly with small numbers of students, and probably with two hundred or so, teachers are able to zero in on the educational process for the limited sample better than those who deal with students in wide and wider geographic regions.

A teacher wants information which can direct student learning in present study as well as data for direction of the teaching-learning process for other groups of students next year and following years. Some information is needed to indicate mastery of a particular, well-defined body of subject matter. Other information will be needed to indicate how well, or to what degree, each student has grasped, learned, or assimilated a general body of subject matter. Other information is needed about each specific student's particular trouble spots. Other information is needed about the level of skill development, both cognitive and psychomotor. Since this book is devoted to tests, the discussion is limited to testing devices, but the reader should not infer that other devices are not important. Much of what is said about tests applies to other devices and procedures and is discussed in a more appropriate place in this series; however, nontesting procedures deserve an equal place with testing in data-collection to supply the information which classroom teachers need to make judgments and decisions about each individual student, groups of students, and school instructional programs.

Classroom teachers need to construct some tests which are tied directly to a set of behavioral objectives—those tests which are criterion referenced. Interpretation of students' scores on the criterion-referenced test is made to an absolute standard established before administration of the test. In general, students who fail to meet the established criterion will be cycled through an instructional period designed to bring each person to mastery of the **standard.**

Classroom teachers need to construct some norm-referenced tests, which are tied to a set of general objectives but not to a predetermined standard. Interpretation of students' scores is made to a norm set by the students. In general, there is no large body of knowledge which everyone is expected to learn in its entirety. The learning is in degree, or amounts, rather than in absolutes. Satisfactory performance is considered to be reached at one minimum, but the tests are built to specifications which allow students to go far beyond the minimum. The tests have a ceiling which will be reached only rarely, if ever.

To further explain the difference between the two systems of score interpretation—criterion-referenced and norm-referenced—the two examples which follow point up the principles of each. A study of first aid must result in each student completely mastering certain skills and knowledge before being assigned to an emergency vehicle to administer to accident victims. Although there is no intention of restricting what the students learn, and certain knowledge beyond the minimum is probably assimilated by each student, the test is built to measure for a clear set of objectives or body of knowledge. The student should score at perfect mastery. None of us wants the person who tends a broken leg for us to know 70% of what s/he needs to know to prepare that leg for a trip in the ambulance. On the other hand, a social studies teacher might feel comfortable that students score at different places in a test for study of Russian history, each one meeting the requirements of satisfactorily fulfilling the objectives, but at different levels. An unsatisfactory performance is possible under norm-referencing, but the decision about performance is made at least in part on how other students performed on the test.

Classroom teachers need to construct some tests which pinpoint where a specific student has a particular difficulty. These tests are needed for diagnosis. Subjects which are in total, or in part, sequential are structured so that future learning depends on certain preceding learning. A difficulty at one point means trouble at another point. For example, a student may not be able to use a division algorithm because s/he can not multiply accurately, subtract properly, place the number in the proper place in the quotient, or one of several other problem points. A test to identify the specific difficulty must be built to function diagnostically. Interpretation of a student's total score may not be as important as the underlying work or computation. Processes used and procedures can reveal points of weaknesses, and some tests are primarily intended to diagnose rather than to measure. In general, those students who make a perfect score are considered to have no weaknesses. Papers from all other students who are considered to have possible problems are scrutinized to diagnose specific trouble and instruction is provided to overcome it.

Classroom teachers need to construct some tests which measure the level of skill development. Since most of these tests do not give a score the same way as a paper-and-pencil test does, interpretation is made differently from other types of classroom tests. In each of the above cases, interpretation of students' scores, although made differently, is in response to the teacher's question of "What did you get?"

STUDENT NEEDS

From the time when teachers begin returning sets of test papers to students, the students' interest about other students' performance is reflected in queries of "Whadjagit?" The student needs to know how others did on the test to make judgment of his/her performance. The student is building a reference system which would allow interpretation of a score relative to other scores. Setting aside the possible element of ego-building for those students who scored high on the test, the major reason for comparison is that of trying to build meaning into a raw score.

A test score is an **index** of measurement which must be given meaning in some way. Additional information is needed to allow meaningful interpretation. For criterion-referenced tests, the score can be compared to the criterion point for minimum acceptance or the set of standards if more than one point is used to set levels of performance. The student probably knew before the test was administered what these standards were, so the frame of reference for interpretation was readily available. For norm-referenced interpretation, several alternatives are available. The teacher should provide an interpretation base and/or record on the students' papers to indicate students' relative performance. The age of the students and their past experience with systems of interpretation will guide the teacher's selection of a reporting scheme.

The following chapters provide the reader with a wide range of alternatives from which to choose. Each of these is based on a simple mathematical principle and explains scores in a particular way. Each one can be used to tell the student what s/he got without the need to ask fellow students "Whadjagit?"

These same procedures are also valuable when comparing a student or class of students to performance of other similar students. This is often done for standardized tests, when scores are compared to a norm or a norm schedule. Teachers also find that a class lesson about how to express scores is pertinent. This method has purpose for the students because it allows the teacher to integrate a mathematical assignment into the school program. Interpretation of students' raw scores according to structured transformations are made to answer the students' questions of "Whadjagit?"

Meaningful Interpretation

The instructional program is designed to bring about change in the student body collectively and students individually. Instructional objectives direct the choice of strategies for the school program and serve as a **sounding board** for evaluation. How do teachers know how much change has been made? How do teachers know in which direction the change was made? These two questions are answerable only through observation of students. To determine behavior change student behavior must be observed.

Observation in the classroom must include more than physical observation made direclty on the one being observed by direct observation by the teacher. It must also probe deeply for information about student achievement, and administration of a test is one way of extending observation beyond direct observation of physical characterics and observable behavior of the students.[2] Historically, crude observation was first used to gather certain information about individual students and classes of students. Even today, most of the observations which teachers make during day-to-day schoolroom events are unrecorded and are interpreted and acted upon in a few seconds. It logically follows that an element of good teaching is the ability to make, interpret, and act upon these unrecorded observations. Recorded observations originating from direct observation and testing procedures are also important for reference by students, teachers, and others when total assessment of students is being formed.

Observation by tests is created to give purposeful direction to generation of data with enough validity to make judgments. Observations of current behavior indicate effectiveness of previous instruction, present status, and aid in predicting future behavior. The importance of interpretation cannot be overestimated.

Test administration is not enough. A properly administered test which has been accurately scored, recorded, and reported is not enough. The score must be given meaning in some way. Although score interpretation contributes to assignment of marks, utilization of the scores should go far beyond that use. The feedback of information to direct

[2] Charles D. Hopkins and Richard L. Antes, *Classroom Measurement and Evaluation* (Itasca, Ill.: F. E. Peacock Publishers, Inc., 1978), pp 54-84.

program revision, decisions for future student study, and future career decisions is the most important function of scores that students make on tests. A good testing program with good score interpretation provides one of the best ways to support effective school instruction. Proper coordination will make the testing program an integral part of the ongoing classroom activities.

CRITERION-REFERENCED INTERPRETATION

Scores on a criterion-referenced test are intended to describe in absolute terms what is meant by each examinee's test performance. Trying to find agreement about what a criterion-referenced test really is can be likened to defining creativity. Creativity is difficult to define because it means different things to different persons, indicating that there may be different kinds of creativity and that it is exhibited in different ways. One of the stronger supporters of criterion-referenced testing, W. James Popham, expresses what he feels will "capture the quintessence of criterion-referenced measurement." He defines it as a test that is used to ascertain an individual's status with respect to a well-defined behavioral domain.[3]

To interpret scores within the above framework, the teacher or other person must have reason to believe that there is a close relationship between the established domain and the behaviors demanded by the items on the test. Since it is not our purpose to discuss test construction here, the assumption is made that this can be done. Devotees to criterion-referenced measurement assure us that scores from well-constructed tests can give a clear description of what the measured performance means. Other equally knowledgeable educators question whether or not this can be done. Using the premise that it can be done, the standard must be set to establish the criterion or **descriptor set** to be used to interpret the scores. Since no one standard can work for all situations, each test must be considered as a special case. A 95 percent rate for passing criterion on a difficult test is a much different standard from a 95 percent rate for passing criterion on an easy test. The use of the test scores will also be needed to make decisions about where to set criterion points for performance interpretation.

Teachers who want to use criterion-refrenced tests face many unanswered questions about setting performance standards. One fact must be kept in mind: minimal acceptance for test performance will be set subjectively. Although as much objectivity as possible must be

[3] W. James Popham, *Criterion-Referenced Measurement* (Englewood Cliffs, N.J.: Prentice-Hall, Inc., 1978, p. 93.

brought to bear on the decision, the final decision will be based on judgment.

Establishing the Criterion

Only when 100% mastery of subject or topic under study is needed is there a clear and well-defined minimum acceptance level for a criterion-referenced test. Since elementary and secondary school students are rarely engaged in study which requires perfect mastery, the design for interpretation must be based on either, past performance of students like those who took this test, or professional knowledge, or both.

How well have students in past years scored on a particular test? Given baseline data and information collected from past administrations, the teacher should be able to set reasonable levels for acceptance. If higher performance is deemed necessary and instructional thrust has been made to improve performance behavior, the teacher could raise the standards whereby student performance will be judged.

If data are not available, the teacher can ask other teachers who have expertise in the topic to help set reasonable levels of expectation for student test behavior. Each contributor should study the behavior domain as defined for the test and individually set a level for the absolute criterion for satisfactory performance. The teachers who made individual decisions about the level could meet collectively and reconcile the estimates needed for criterion into a single performance level to be used in interpreting the scores. When that standard is set, then each student's score is compared to that score and is judged as meeting criterion (passing) or not meeting criterion (not passing).

Errors in Decisions

A factor which must be considered when setting levels for acceptable performance is the seriousness of making certain decision errors. Which is more serious: advance a student to further study (consider a study completed) when s/he should not be advanced, or mistakenly hold a student for further study when s/he should be advanced?

To protect against the first error (Type I) of mistaken advancement, the teacher would set the standard for passing very high. To protect against the second error (Type II) of mistaken retention for further study, the teacher would lower the standard for passing. Since it is not known for sure whether pass or fail is correct, there is always a possible error attached with each decision, and the seriousness of one error compared to the other error must be considered. For example, the first-aid instructor would set a very high standard for passing criterion to

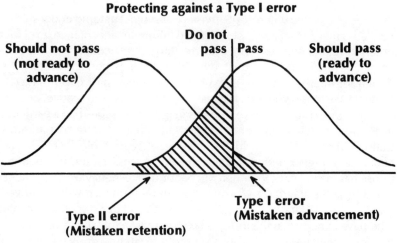

Part A
Protecting against a Type I error

Should not pass (not ready to advance)

Do not pass | **Pass**

Should pass (ready to advance)

Type II error (Mistaken retention)

Type I error (Mistaken advancement)

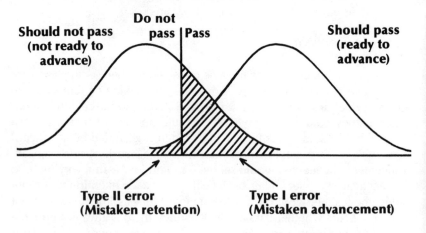

Part B
Protecting against a Type II error

Should not pass (not ready to advance)

Do not pass | **Pass**

Should pass (ready to advance)

Type II error (Mistaken retention)

Type I error (Mistaken advancement)

Figure 3.2 Relationship of decision errors.

protect against sending incompetent attendents in emergency vehicles. Some competent students might be sacrificed to protect against a Type I error as illustrated in Part A of Figure 3.2. A social studies teacher who teaches Russian history would probably not set criterion levels as high because the Type I error is not as serious as a Type II error because it is not so crucial that s/he protect against mistaken advancement. More harm might be made in mistaken retention, so the level is lowered as illustrated in Part B of Figure 3.2.

The decision requires careful consideraton about possible consequences of each type of errors. Hopefully, errors of both kinds can be minimized in real-world decisions based on criterion-referenced interpretation of student scores.

NORM-REFERENCED INTERPRETATION

A score on a norm-referenced test is intended to describe a student's test performance in relationship to others who took the test at the same time (same class) or to others whose scores are used to establish external criteria for performance levels on a wide scale. Students who ask classmates "Whadjagit?" are using a form of norm referencing as they try to establish some sort of reference system to interpret a raw score that has been marked on a paper. The reporting systems described in the following three chapters are merely sophisticated versions of the student's approach. Unless a criterion-referenced test, a mastery test, or a problem test is used, some indication of relative standing should be reported to a student in addition to the raw score. In addition, administrators and other teachers, as well as classroom teachers, need measures of relative standing to aid in score interpretation.

Establishing the Norm

When the use of the scores directs the teacher to norm-referenced interpretation, a decision must be made about how to report performance. Many reporting systems are available, and each has certain advantages and also disadvantages. Which reporting system to be used is selected by giving consideration to (1) who is to receive the data and (2) how the person will be using the data. Since more than one person may be using the data, it is conceivable that more than one system may be needed to satisfy everyone involved. When external norm groups are used for interpretation, standard scores (see Chapter 5) and percentile bands (see Chapter 6) may be the best way to report student performance on tests to administration persons. Students and parents might understand graphical representations (see Chapter 4) or stanines (see Chapter 6) better. If there is any question about whether or not the person receiving the information will understand the scheme, then an explanation should accompany the report. If students understand standard scores, the report could be one of the standard scores reported as z or Z (see Chapter 5).

A schoolwide reporting of scores on classroom tests as Z-scores allows a common reference system which is standard for test scores in the school. Use of a schoolwide reporting system is encouraged because of the uniformity it gives to scores on classroom paper-and-pencil tests. Even if the school does not use the system, a teacher can give uniformity to tests throughout his or her teaching by adopting Z-scores as a reporting base, thus giving an interpretation base which is the same for all tests given in that classroom. This does not mean that the same score always means the same thing on all occasions. It does give a specific place in the raw-score distribution without getting involved in the characteristics of each distribution. This concept will be clearer to the reader after study of the next chapter.

If external norms are used, the teacher will probably have tables which allow a direct comparison of each score to the norm-group performance. The tables were developed by using one or more of the reporting systems' calculations for all possible test scores and listing the raw scores in one column and the associated norm scores in another column. Figure 3.3 gives a reporting scheme for percentile ranks for raw scores from a score of one to the highest possible score of 90. Most tests which are normed will have tables for several different reporting systems so that interpretations can be made to fit the needs of the consumer of the test data.

Using Norms

The teacher has much freedom to choose ways to report student performance scores since there are several norming systems available. Each of the norming systems uses a different approach, so each has certain unique characteristics. After studying the next three chapters, your repertory of systems to select from can be used to report scores from tests constructed by you and administered to your students.

Selection of the system to use for specific classroom tests must be made carefully, taking into consideration how much the students know about the several different techniques. Arithmetical averages are probably the easiest to understand, and the first reporting may be in terms of average, below average, or above average. Although this may be a crude reporting, it does give the person a frame of reference with which to interpret the raw score. A next step may be to use the stanine distribution to report a raw score performance. A stanine reporting system has the

Raw Score	\<Level 3–6 Grade PR's\> 3	4	5	6	Raw Score	Raw Score	\<Level 3–6 Grade PR's\> 3	4	5	6	Raw Score
90					90	40	72	43	22	12	40
89					89	39	70	41	21	12	39
88				99	88	38	69	40	20	11	38
87				98	87	37	67	39	19	11	37
86			99	96	86	36	66	37	18	10	36
85			98	94	85	35	64	36	17	10	35
84			98	92	84	34	63	35	16	9	34
83			97	89	83	33	61	33	15	8	33
82			96	87	82	32	59	32	14	8	32
81			94	84	81	31	58	30	13	7	31
80			93	81	80	30	55	28	12	6	30
79		99	91	78	79	29	53	27	12	6	29
78		98	90	75	78	28	51	25	11	6	28
77		98	88	72	77	27	49	24	10	5	27
76		97	86	69	76	26	47	22	9	5	26
75		97	84	66	75	25	45	20	8	5	25
74		96	82	63	74	24	43	19	8	4	24
73		95	80	60	73	23	41	18	7	4	23
72		94	78	57	72	22	38	16	6	3	22
71		94	75	54	71	21	36	15	5	3	21
70		93	73	52	70	20	33	13	5	3	20
69	99	92	71	50	69	19	30	12	4	2	19
68	99	90	68	48	68	18	27	11	3	2	18
67	98	89	66	46	67	17	24	9	3	1	17
66	98	87	63	44	66	16	21	8	2	1	16
65	97	86	61	42	65	15	18	7	2		15
64	97	84	59	40	64	14	16	6	1		14
63	96	83	57	38	63	13	14	5	1		13
62	96	81	55	36	62	12	12	4			12
61	95	79	53	34	61	11	9	3			11
60	95	77	51	33	60	10	8	3			10
59	94	75	49	31	59	9	6	2			9
58	93	74	47	29	58	8	5	2			8
57	92	72	45	28	57	7	4	1			7
56	91	70	44	27	56	6	3				6
55	90	68	42	25	55	5	2				5
54	89	66	40	24	54	4	1				4
53	88	64	38	23	53	3					3
52	87	63	37	22	52	2					2
51	86	61	35	21	51	1					1
50	85	59	34	20	50						
49	84	57	32	19	49						
48	82	55	31	18	48						
47	81	54	30	17	47						
46	80	52	29	16	46						
45	79	50	28	15	45						
44	77	48	27	15	44						
43	76	47	26	14	43						
42	75	45	24	14	42						
41	73	44	23	13	41						

Figure 3.3 Percentile ranks of raw scores by grade and test level.

SOURCE: Charles D. Hopkins and Richard L. Antes, *Classroom Measurement and Evaluation* (Itasca, Ill.: F. E. Peacock Publishers, Inc., 1978), p. 384.

advantage of interpretation to broad categories without the involvement of small differences. The person being reported to does not have to understand the mathematical principles, so a stanine tells parents and young children in broad terms how well the student's score stands in relationship to other students.

Students should be introduced to a standard score distribution as soon as possible. By the fourth or fifth grade (earlier for some students and groups of students), the arithmetical average and the standard deviation should be presented to students. With that background, the basic z-score can be developed. A lesson on the characteristics of the normal curve allows the student to interpret the standard scores with knowledge of the area of the curve. This is explained in the next chapter. Elementary school teachers have found that this study allows expansion of the mathematics program beyond the usual course of study and that these are rather sophisticated principles that most students of this age can understand.

A percentile rank is easy to explain to students since it uses the concept of percentage which most students at the intermediate level or above understand. Parents also understand percentile-rank interpretation. Graphical representation of score distributions can be made, and then each student's score can be shown (see Figure 3.4) on a copy of the graph.

In general, measurement (physical, psychological, as well as educational) is conducted to determine the amount of something. Thermometers give readings which allow interpretation of the amount of heat in the air or some object. An engineer's steel tape and steel rule are devices to measure distance and length. Other devices are constructed to give a numerical description to some specific attribute. Norm-referenced tests are designed to generate scores which measure an attribute in such a way that scores indicate relative amounts of that attribute. Satisfactory interpretation of scores one to another is therefore made by explaining relationships through a reporting scheme which goes beyond assessing performance as meeting minimum requirements or not. In this way the score should carry more information since the test is built to measure at all points on the scale and should serve to answer questions of "What did you get?" or "Whadjagit?"

DIAGNOSTIC INTERPRETATION

The use of tests for diagnostic purposes is primarily at the classroom level. For a test to give information of a diagnostic nature, it must reveal specific difficulties or weaknesses that students have in learning, study, or skill development. To some extent, any test used for

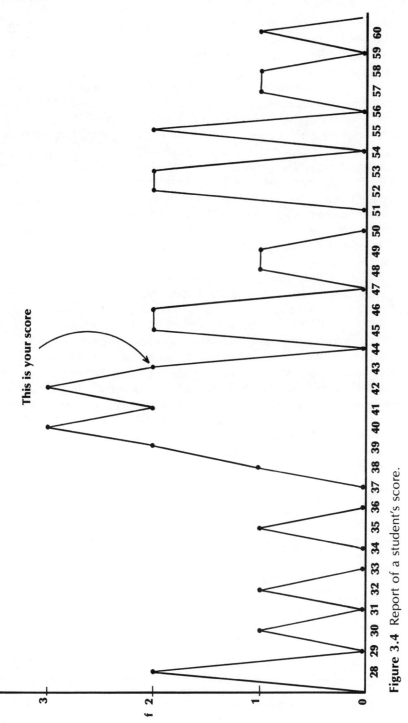

Figure 3.4 Report of a student's score.

measurement can be diagnostic because missed items could be considered trouble spots. However, to be truly diagnostic, a test should be constructed to point up specific deficiencies with little or no component of measurement per se.

Examples of diagnostic tests are devices which are used for identification of learning disabilities.[4] Each test is designed to point out one or more disabilities that a student may have. For example, a widely used test[5] for early learners assesses basic concepts considered to be essential for success in school. They are grouped into four categories: (1) spatial concepts, (2) quantitative concepts, (3) temporal concepts, and (4) miscellaneous concepts—different, other, alike, matches. The level of development for each of the four concepts is interpreted by looking at a series of responses for a set of the items which relates to one of the four groups. The total number of pass, or correct, items provides an indication of the child's overall knowledge of the four concepts but nothing about specific weaknesses.

Teachers who want to diagnose student weaknesses may find published tests to serve the classroom needs. If they are not available, the teacher may need to design tests to perform the diagnosis.

The task in building a diagnostic test is much the same in principle to the automobile mechanic who structures probes into specific places of a car's engine and associated parts when trouble shooting an automobile's mechanical failure. The teacher must know where to probe and how to pick up signals from student responses.[6] Interpretation of students' responses involves how the student reacted to the set of items which relate to a concept. The teacher is the one who asks, "What did you get?" after a diagnostic test. S/he expects to be able to direct each specific student to a set of activities which will overcome the deficiencies that have been identified from the results of the test.

INTERPRETATION OF SKILL DEVELOPMENT

The ongoing, everyday activities in classrooms require teachers to use many techniques to assess progress of students. Some

[4] Charles D. Hopkins and Richard L. Antes, "Screening for Identification of Learning Disabilities," in *Classroom Measurement and Evaluation* (Itasca, Ill.: F. E. Peacock Publishers, Inc., 1978), pp. 391-413.

[5] Anne E. Boehm, *Boehm Test of Basic Concepts* (New York: Psychological Corporation, 1970).

[6] For help in building diagnostic tests, see J. Stanley Ahmann and Marvin D. Glock, "Diagnosis and Remediation of Problems," in *Evaluating Pupil Growth,* 5th ed. (Boston: Allyn and Bacon, Inc., 1975), pp. 342-66.

objectives are directed specifically to skill development. The skill may be development largely within the cognitive domain such as oral reading, it may be skill development largely within the psychomotor domain, such as welding, or a skill which relies heavily on a combination of the two domains, such as typing. For skill development or the procedural aspects of performance, the purpose of interpretation will be to identify where a sequence is broken or a procedure does not conform to accepted aspects of process.

Interpretation of skill development is made to a set of established standards. In general, interpretation of skill development is a form of criterion-referenced interpretaton. Each teacher, using professional knowledge and help of other knowledgeable persons, must establish a standard or set of standards for student performance to serve as a comparison for the collected data. In some cases, such as individualzed programs, realistic criteria are established for a specific student.

Tests for skill development may or may not have scores to be interpreted. In general, a score will not be the most important aspect in making an assessment. The interpretation may be much like that used in diagnostic testing, where the teacher looks to specifics rather than to an overall total score. Checklists, rating scales, mechanical devices, ranking, scorecards, and product scales are widely used in assessment of skill development.[7] Some of these generate total scores, but the worth of the device can be found in analysis of the components that make up the total rather than the total itself.

Skill development cannot be completely isolated from other aspects of expectations, and the teacher must recognize that skill development always involves an element of cognitive aspects of human functioning. For example, how would you classify essay or theme writing? Some persons see this as nearly a pure cognitive functioning, while others define it as primarily exhibition of a skill. The question asked of students who are being assessed as to skill development becomes "What were you able to do?" and interpretation is made with regard to student performance as it compares to standards.

Judgments and Decisions

Any model or scheme that is to explain the process of education will include a component devoted to assessment. Any model for assessment or evaluation will have a component which allows for judgments to be formed. Another common component for such models is

[7]Charles D. Hopkins and Richard L. Antes, *Classroom Measurement and Evaluation* (Itasca, Ill.: F. E. Peacock Publishers, Inc., 1978), pp. 313-40.

devoted to decision making. The collection of information is not the end but, rather, a means to an end. Judgments are based on information collected, and decisions, in turn, rely on the judgments. If a question is to be answered with a statement about what now exists or about how a student will perform in the future, then a judgment is being asked for. If a question is to be answered by a statement about certain action to be taken (school program changes or student assignment), then a decision is being asked for.

FORMING JUDGMENTS

The importance of learning how to reduce information into valid judgments cannot be overemphasized. Reading essay responses, diagnosing problems, assigning marks, and predicting future performance are all examples of judgments that teachers are required to make. Much of what was said about scoring in Chapter 2 and discussion about interpreting scores relates either directly or indirectly to making judgments. Clearly, testing makes much more of a contribution than generation of a score to be written as a record for future reference.

Being aware of the fact that test scores contribute to the bank of information that will be needed to form judgments will help the teacher to be conscious of the importance of the evaluation process. This awareness should result in better judgments, and an understanding of the process should produce better input for decisions. The details of making judgments go beyond this study and may be found in other sources. The presentation in the sections which precede this section, common sense, and professional understanding should prepare a teacher to work out the details for effective classroom evaluation until s/he has the time and/or opportunity to study that topic in depth. The best procedure to use is to form judgments (evaluation) on the broadest base of information that can be collected and to include data from tests and information from non-testing procedures. Judgments can be verified by checking the accuracy of the information and supporting empirical evidence.

MAKING DECISIONS

Decision making is such a common duty, especially for teachers, that it is often done with little or no formal consideration to process. Decisions are made routinely in the course of day-to-day events, and good teaching rests on being able to act on a unique set of circumstances without taking time out to apply a decision-making model. However, many decisions should be carefully carried out through a systematic process.

The first consideration to be given to a system for decision-making is that basic judgments must be verified. Often the difference between a valid decision and a faulty one is that the first is arrived at scientifically. A scientific approach generates decisions based on observed events and a rational attempt to interpret them. Science uses data-based explanations to provide the best decision at that time. A decision is not guaranteed correct but the most likely decision to be true given the evidence at hand. A teacher must be intellectually honest, making no decisions on the basis of faith, power, monetary rewards, self-protection, or without verified judgment.

Decisions about students and school programs can be made within the following five step process:

1. **State what you want to accomplish. (Specific objective)**
2. **Isolate each possible alternative. (Possibilities)**
3. **Consider all verified judgments. (Strengths)**
4. **Weigh the consequences for each possible alternative. (Probable outcomes)**
5. **Select the alternative that seems to be most appropriate. (Best action)**

For an individual, the decision process is very specific, but for decisions about programs the scope of the decision process is very broad. As with most processes, when explanation is given in steps, the spirit of the process is lost, and in practice the steps may not appear in the order given or more than one step may be considered at the same time. Also this list has reduced a very involved process to a few simplified steps. However, if approaches to all decisions are made with consideration of the system, the returns through better school programs and better prepared students are likely to be high.

4 Visual Interpretation

Visual interpretation of test data is helpful to students, parents, school personnel, and other members of the community. Test data carry much more meaningful information when communication includes some form of total performance. In addition to reporting a **raw score** and certain statistics to a student, a visual interpretation gives the reader a quick overview of important characteristics of the distribution of scores, allowing interpretation of one score to total performance.

The frequency distribution, which permits an orderly arrangement of scores from lowest to highest and the frequency with which each score appears, provides a visual picture for the reader. The frequency distribution can be presented in tabular or graphic form. Tables are convenient for calculation procedures and for those persons who have been accustomed to interpreting score distributions. Graphs are especially helpful when reporting to students and parents about school performance. The classification form and description of the scores generates the information which the numbers contain. By inspecting a distribution of scores, the teacher can form judgments not only of general test performance but also some indications of how well the test served as a measuring device.

Frequency Distribution

A general science test was administered to a class and scored. The raw scores appeared as follows:

Judy	60	Margaret	58	Brenda	53
Jim	30	Daniel	57	John	40
Chris	39	David	42	Jill	46
Lisa	46	Shelia	35	Kathy	48

Stefanie	28	Carole	55	Ruth	49
Charles	45	Lynne	39	Scott	42
Elaine	32	Ralph	28	Kim	43
Stacey	43	Rita	45	Bill	40
Susan	38	Lorie	52	Holly	52
Steve	40	Tiffany	42	Rich	53

A visual inspection of the 30 scores provides little information about how well the class did on the test or the relationship of one score to the others. What can be gained by scanning the list of raw scores are: (1) the highest score is 60 and (2) the lowest score is 28. One quick and simple way to discern more information is to arrange the scores in order of decreasing magnitude as shown in Figure 4.1. Ordering the

Name	Raw Score X	Rank
Judy	60	1
Margaret	58	2
Daniel	57	3
Carole	55	4
Brenda	53	5.5
Rich	53	5.5
Lorie	52	7.5
Holly	52	7.5
Ruth	49	9
Kathy	48	10
Jill	46	11.5
Lisa	46	11.5
Charles	45	13.5
Rita	45	13.5
Stacey	43	15.5
Kim	43	15.5
David	42	18
Tiffany	42	18
Scott	42	18
Bill	40	21
John	40	21
Steve	40	21
Lynne	39	23.5
Chris	39	23.5
Susan	38	25
Shelia	35	26
Elaine	32	27
Jim	30	28
Ralph	28	29.5
Stefanie	28	29.5

Figure 4.1 Listing of the general science test scores from the highest to the lowest score and associated ranks.

scores by placing each score in its relative position from highest to lowest shows it in its relationship to all other scores. For example, the raw score of 58 was second highest, or the raw score of 32 was the fourth score from the bottom. Other visual interpretations such as these can be made but in general terms only. Placing the name of each student along side of his/her obtained score provides a view of how each student ranked in the class. The relative position of each score in the group may be obtained by assigning a rank to each score. (See Figure 4.1.) All scores are ranked with the highest being assigned a rank of 1, the second a rank of 2, and so on until all scores have been assigned a rank number. Ranks for tied scores are assigned the average rank of the tied series. Individual performance compared to general group performance may be reported by listing a

X	Tallies	f
60	/	1
59		
58	/	1
57	/	1
56		
55	/	1
54		
53	//	2
52	//	2
51		
50		
49	/	1
48	/	1
47		
46	//	2
45	//	2
44		
43	//	2
42	///	3
41		
40	///	3
39	//	2
38	/	1
37		
36		
35	/	1
34		
33		
32	/	1
31		
30	/	1
29		
28	//	2
Total		N = 30

Figure 4.2 Consecutively numbered scores with the tallies and frequency of the scores.

student's rank and the number of students being ranked. For example, Ruth's raw score of 49 would be reported as a rank of 9 out of 30.

A frequency distribution is a systematic arrangement of scores in a series of intervals showing the number of students who had scores in each of the intervals. The steps, listed below, that are taken to set up a frequency distribution for the general science scores are reflected in Figure 4.2:

1. **Find the highest score and the lowest score, and number consecutively from the highest through the lowest score in a column headed "X". The "X" represents the raw scores.**
2. **Head the second column "Tallies," and record a slash or tally mark for each score. If a score value appears twice, this column will have two slashes, three values three slashes, and so on.**
3. **In the third column count the slash marks, and place the number corresponding to the total number of tallies for each raw-score value. The "f" column represents the frequency of each score's occurrence.**
4. **Sum the "f" column, and record the number of scores (N) as a total.**

If the scores have previously been arranged in sequential order, an alternative way to get the frequencies for the scores is by listing only those scores actually obtained on the test. Figure 4.3 illustrates how a table would be set up if an ordering of scores had previously been made.

When the interval between the lowest and highest score values exceeds about 20, grouping scores into intervals may aid analysis. When teachers are reporting test scores to parents, administrators, and citizens of the community for a very large class or for one or more classes, the grouped frequency distribution may be helpful. Grouped data condense the scores into a smaller number of categories which may aid in interpretation of a large number of scores or a set of scores with a wide range. This kind of grouping also aids in the visual representations in graphs. The characteristic shape of a graph is usually more apparent if the data have been grouped. Sets of scores can be reported easily to students in the classroom by using raw score values without grouping, especially since hand calculators expedite calculations. The steps in arranging the general science test scores into a grouped frequency distribution are as follows (example in Figure 4.4):

1. **Determine the range of scores. The range is the difference between the highest and lowest scores. In the set of test scores the highest score is 60 and the lowest is 28. The range is 32. [If range = $(X_H - X_L) + 1$, then the range = 33.]**
2. **Divide the range by 10 and 20. About 10 to 20 intervals are used for grouped frequency distributions.**
3. **Determine the size of the class interval to be used. In this**

X	Tallies	f	cf
60	/	1	30
58	/	1	29
57	/	1	28
55	/	1	27
53	//	2	26
52	//	2	24
49	/	1	22
48	/	1	21
46	//	2	20
45	//	2	18
43	//	2	16
42	///	3	14
40	///	3	11
39	//	2	8
38	/	1	6
35	/	1	5
32	/	1	4
30	/	1	3
28	//	2	2

Figure 4.3 Tabular representation of the test scores in a frequency distribution.

Interval	Tallies	f	cf
60–62	/	1	30
57–59	//	2	29
54–56	/	1	27
51–53	////	4	26
48–50	//	2	22
45–47	////	4	20
42–44	⫽//	5	16
39–41	⫽//	5	11
36–38	/	1	6
33–35	/	1	5
30–32	//	2	4
27–29	//	2	2

Figure 4.4 Grouped frequency distribution of thirty general science test scores.

example of test scores, dividing the range of 32 by 10 gives 3.2. Dividing 32 by 20 gives 1.6. The size of the interval should be between the two values just determined, and should be an odd number. For this example, 3 is an appropriate interval size.

4. Identify the lowest score in the distribution. In this example, 28 is the lowest score.

5. Establish a lowest interval that includes the lowest score, 28. Select the lower limit of the interval by finding the multiple of the interval size just below the lowest score. For example, 27 (9 x 3) is the next multiple of 3 below 28. The lowest score is

28, and the interval width is 3, and a score of 27, which is a multiple of 3, is closest to 28. Consequently, 27 is used as the lower limit of the lowest interval, 27–29. Continue listing the intervals, 30–32, 33–35, and so on until the interval which includes the highest score is reached. For this distribution that interval is 60–62.

6. Tally each raw score according to the interval in which it falls. The frequency of each interval is the number of scores which fall within the interval as indicated by the tallies. The sum of the *f*(frequency) column gives the total number of scores.

A comparison of Figures 4.1, 4.2, and 4.3 with 4.4 provides a visual illustration of the advantage of grouping when dealing with a set of scores that has a large range. With the 30 scores used in these figures, one can readily view how the data are condensed through grouping procedures for score presentation since the frequency distribution is based on a grouping employing 15 intervals that span the range of scores. For example, if 80 scores were concentrated in the same score range, they would also be grouped into approximately 15 intervals for presentation purposes.

The individuality of each score is lost in the grouping process, and the interval represents the scores included within it. Viewing Figure 4.4, one can see that the interval 51-53 includes four scores, although the number value of each of the four scores is unknown, except that there is a combination of 51, 52, and 53 score values. From Figure 4.3 one can see that the score value of 51 did not occur, 52 occurred two times, and 53 occurred two times, which provides the frequency of four which appears in Figure 4.4. A visual representation through a histogram or frequency polygon illustrates the loss of individuality more vividly.

Histogram

The histogram is a graph of a distribution of scores or frequency distribution prepared by placing the test score values on a horizontal axis, or baseline, with the scores increasing in magnitude from left to right. The scale for the vertical axis on the left side of the graph is used to indicate frequency of occurrence—the number of students earning each score. The vertical axis begins with 0 and moves to the highest frequency appearing for any score. The data on a histogram are shown in the form of rectangular columns. The width of the base of each rectangle represents the score(s) as an interval, and the height represents the number of students falling within the interval. Figure 4.5 is a histogram of the achievement scores from the general science test. Figure 4.6 presents the grouped scores for the same test in the form of a histogram. The histogram of the grouped scores uses the limits of each interval as the

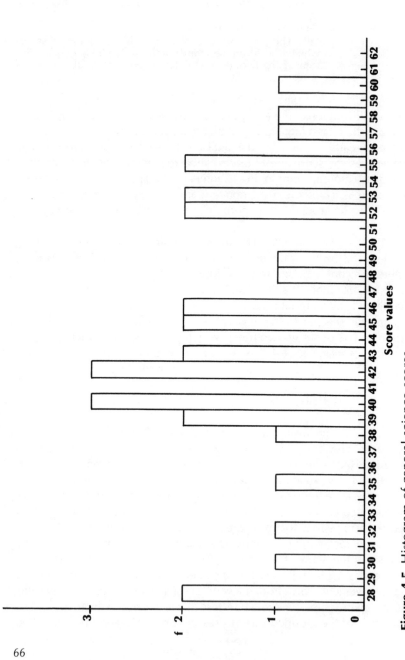

Figure 4.5 Histogram of general science scores.

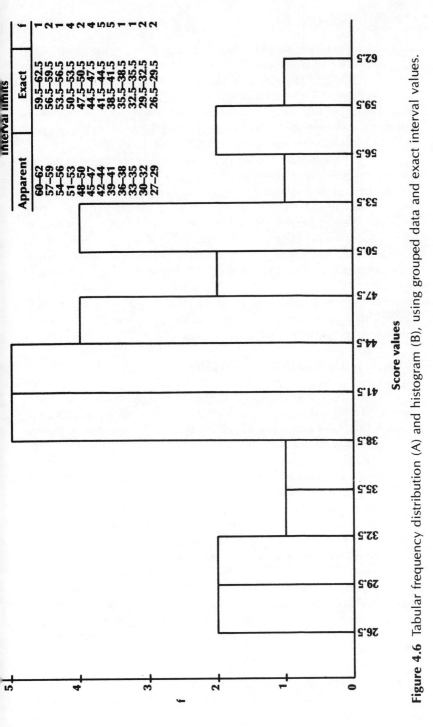

Figure 4.6 Tabular frequency distribution (A) and histogram (B), using grouped data and exact interval values.

points along the baseline of the graph. The apparent score limits of the
interval 27-29 contains scores 27, 28, 29. The interval actually extends
from the point 26.5 to point 29.5, the next interval commences at 29.5
and extends to 32.5, the next from 32.5 to 35.5, and so on. These interval
limits are called true limits, exact limits, or real limits. The real limits
determine the lower and upper limits of each interval. In this way, all
points on the baseline are accounted for in the histogram.

The reader should note that the histogram (also the frequency polygon) drawn from grouped data no longer reflects the portion
of the scores as they appear in the original frequency distribution. Each
score is now associated with a greater baseline interval; thus, some
information about the original scores is lost. However, the advantage of
the grouped-score histogram is that the general characteristics of the
distribution are more apparent after scores have been grouped especially
if the number of observations is relatively small. Although grouping of
scores for calculation is not used widely, since the hand calculator has
become so commonplace, grouping for graphical representation is advantageous and continues to serve as an excellent way to show how a
particular score relates to all other scores.

Frequency Polygon

A frequency distribution presented as a series of points
connected with a series of lines is known as a frequency polygon. It is
different from the histogram in that it is based on the assumption that the
frequencies in each interval are concentrated at the middle of the interval. The frequency polygon is constructed by locating the midpoint of
each interval and recording a dot to represent the number of scores falling
in that interval. Each point would be at the center of the top of one of the
rectangles in the histogram. Figure 4.7 illustrates the relationship between the plotting of the grouped scores for the histogram and a frequency polygon. The frequency polygon is superimposed on the
histogram from Figure 4.6. In the development of a frequency polygon,
the horizontal and vertical scales are laid off exactly as for a histogram.
For each interval a point is located directly above the middle of the
interval. Notice that a point is placed on the line to represent the zero
frequency for the next lower interval and the next higher interval. Figure
4.8 represents the frequency polygon of the ungrouped general science
scores, while Figure 4.9 is the frequency polygon for the grouped data.

The frequency polygon is a graphical representation of a
frequency distribution, and it aids the understanding of the characteristics of the distribution through visual representations of the frequency of scores associated with designated points on the baseline. The

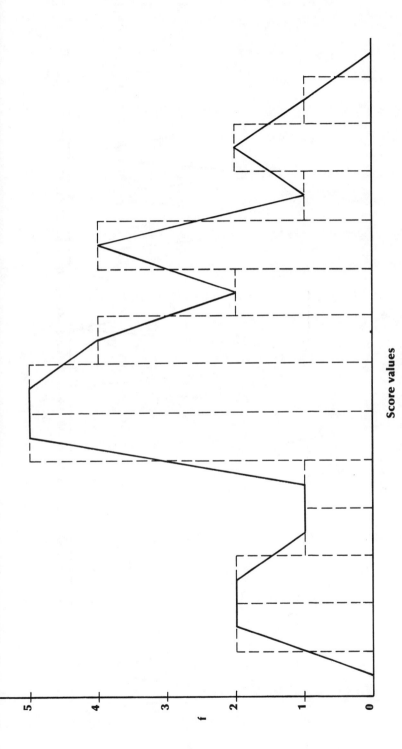

Figure 4.7 Frequency polygon superimposed on a histogram for the same data.

69

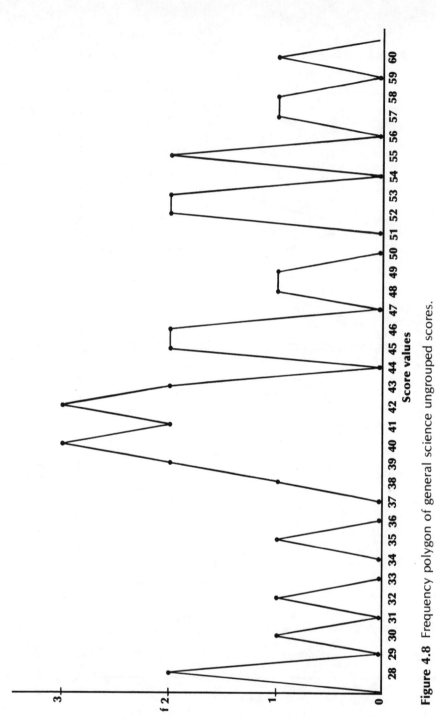

Figure 4.8 Frequency polygon of general science ungrouped scores.

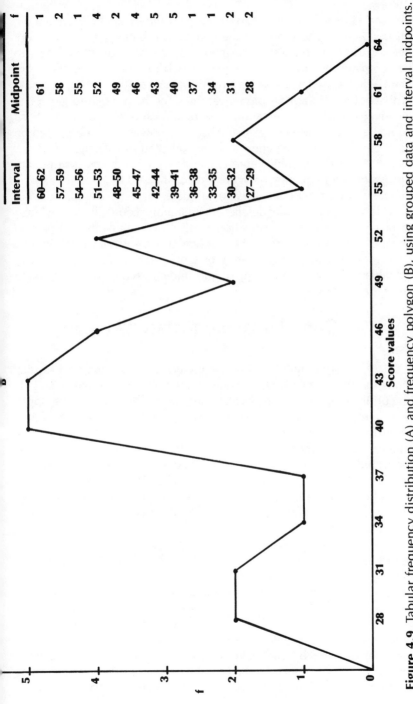

Interval	Midpoint	f
60–62	61	1
57–59	58	2
54–56	55	1
51–53	52	4
48–50	49	2
45–47	46	4
42–44	43	5
39–41	40	5
36–38	37	1
33–35	34	1
30–32	31	2
27–29	28	2

Figure 4.9 Tabular frequency distribution (A) and frequency polygon (B), using grouped data and interval midpoints.

71

physical form of the frequency distribution is widely used to present score distributions and to represent theoretical distributions. Comparison of one score to the group is useful in interpretation. If two distributions are to be compared by graphs, the frequency polygon, rather than the histogram, will be used. Comparing two histograms on the same grid would probably result in a mass of vertical lines and be difficult to glean any meaning from the presentation. The relationship of two distributions could be better presented as two frequency polygons superimposed on each other, and interpretation will be facilitated (See Figure 4.16.)

The graphic representations of a frequency distribution, histogram and frequency polygon, are constructed to give the reader a picture for a quick visual analysis of test data. Although a graph does not provide an opportunity for detailed examination, it does allow the viewer to place a single value in relation to all others. Students and parents generally are more concerned about how a score is related to the total results rather than to particular other scores, and a graph is especially valuable to reveal the meaning of one student's score compared to the group performance.

Cumulative Frequency Polygon

The cumulative frequency polygon uses the upper exact limits and the cumulative frequencies for the set of scores being plotted. The ordinate is used for the frequencies and the abscissa for the upper limits. Before a cumulative frequency polygon can be plotted, the scores of the distribution must be added serially or cumulated. In Figure 4.4, the f column indicates the frequency of scores for each interval. To determine the cumulative frequency (cf) the frequencies are added from the f column as follows: the first cumulative frequency is 2; 2 + 2 gives 4, the second cumulative frequency; 4 + 1 gives 5, the third cumulative frequency. The last cumulative frequency totals 30, equal to N (number of scores).

The cumulative-frequency polygon shows the number of scores less than an upper-limit score value. For example, for Figure 4.10 the score value of 62.5 has 30 scores below it. Using the scale on the right of Figure 4.10, percentages of scores falling below specific points (percentile ranks) can be read directly from the graph with reasonable accuracy. Also the score which indicates a point where a specific percentage of scores fall below (percentiles) can also be read directly. Percentile ranks can be found by reading from the score on the abscissa vertically to the polygon then right horizontally to the percentage. To find percentiles read from the ordinate to the polygon and down to the score value.

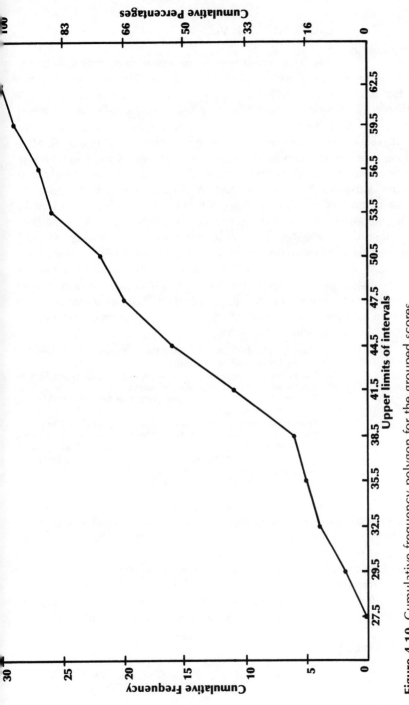

Figure 4.10 Cumulative frequency polygon for the grouped scores.

73

Normal Curve

The normal distribution is a type of frequency distribution which many sets of data tend to approximate. The normal frequency distribution is a smoothed polygon called the normal curve. It is a theoretical distribution based on an infinite number of values that vary symmetrically. The normal curve is not a distribution of actual scores but a theoretical distribution plotted from a mathematical equation. Measures from many human characteristics and scores from most norm-referenced tests yield distributions which approximate the normal curve. Many **variables** dealt with in testing are considered to be normally distributed, and the normal curve presents a model distribution for interpretation of scores of most groups on most tests. Many of the methods of obtaining meaningful scores in norm-referenced testing generate scores related to the dimensions and characteristics of the normal curve.

The normal curve is useful in providing a common basis for understanding and interpreting the relationship between different types of scores used to report test results. The properties of the normal curve are known and used to interpret many kinds of test scores. Some of the properties of the normal curve are:

1. **The curve is bell shaped, and the left and right halves are mirror images of each other.**
2. **The curve is symmetrical. The scores or measures are distributed symmetrically around the mean.**
3. **The area under the curve represents the total frequency (N) of the distribution.**
4. **Two points of change of direction (inflection) of the curve occur at the points ±1σ from the mean, and the interval range between these two points includes 68.26 percent of the area under the curve, ±2σ from the mean includes 95.44 percent of the area under the curve, and ±3σ from the mean includes nearly all the area under the curve.**

The shape of the frequency polygon which approximates the normal distribution is illustrated by Figure 4.11, which consists of a histogram and frequency polygon built from a set of scores with a very large N. The important characteristics of the shape of the curve have been pointed out, although the symmetry and degree of peakedness are similar to the normal curve and should be noted. Distributions of test scores or other data can vary from the normal curve on certain characteristics. Skewness and kurtosis are discussed in the next two sections.

SKEWNESS

When scores tend to center around one point, with those on both sides of that point balancing each other (see Figure 4.12), the

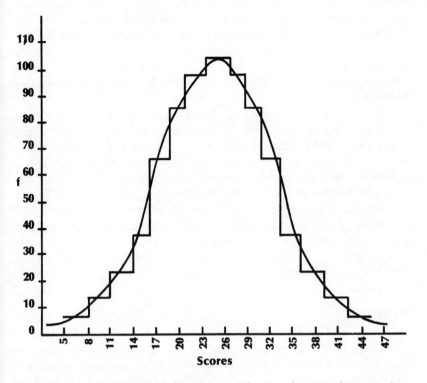

Figure 4.11 Histogram and frequency polygon of a set of scores that closely approximate the characteristics of the normal curve.

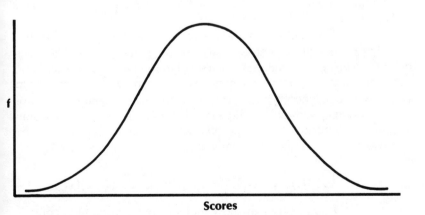

Figure 4.12 Symmetrical frequency polygon (no skewness).

distribution has no skewness, and the shape of the curve is symmetrical. If there are some atypical scores that make the distribution asymmetrical, then the distribution is said to be skewed. If the atypical scores are high values (in the positive direction), the distribution is said to be positively skewed (see Figure 4.13). If the atypical scores are low values (in the negative direction), the distribution is said to be negatively skewed (see Figure 4.14).

The skewness of a distribution of scores is important in interpreting a set of scores to a class, since the reason for the skewness can explain something about the group tested and/or the test itself. In norm-referenced testing, when the scores in a distribution pile up at a relatively low score and tail out for frequencies of higher scores (positively skewed), then the test was too difficult for the students. If scores pile up near the top of the scale and then tail out for frequencies of relatively low scores (negatively skewed), the test may have been too easy for the group. In general, scores from a norm-referenced test should be symmetrical, but that property alone does not indicate whether or not a test is good or poor. Criterion-referenced mastery tests should generate negatively skewed distributions.

KURTOSIS

The characteristic of kurtosis is very closely related to the variability, or spread, of scores from the average score. Kurtosis can give an indication of the degree of homogeneity of the group being tested in regard to the characteristic being measured. If students tend to be much alike, the scores will generate a leptokurtic frequency polygon as represented by A in Figure 4.15, and if students are very different, a platykurtic distribution as represented by B in Figure 4.15. A mesokurtic distribution is neither platykurtic nor leptokurtic and is represented by C in Figure 4.15.

If a set of scores produces a leptokurtic frequency distribution, then the conclusion can be drawn that the group was homogeneous on the trait that the test measured. If a set of scores produces a platykurtic frequency distribution, then the conclusion to be drawn is that the group was very heterogeneous on the trait that the test measured. If a set of scores produces a mesokurtic frequency distribution, then the conclusion to be drawn is that the group was heterogeneous on the trait and that the trait was distributed about normally in the population measured.

Using Graphs in the Classroom

Using graphs to show relationships among test scores is helpful in conveying the meaning of data. Most graphs represent numbers

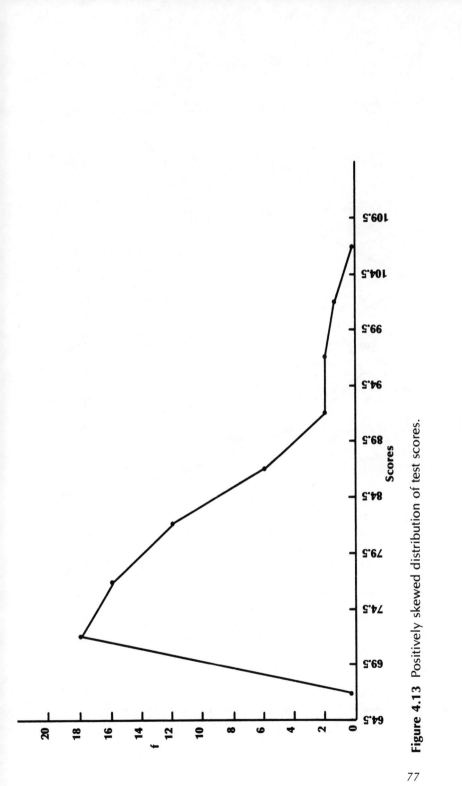

Figure 4.13 Positively skewed distribution of test scores.

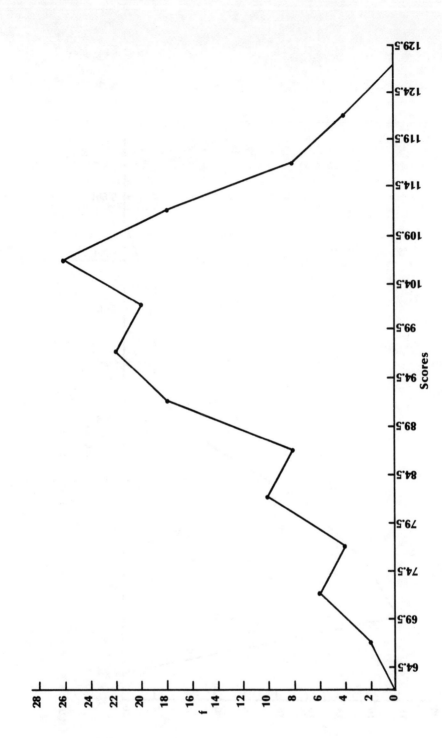

Figure 4.14 Negatively skewed distribution of test scores.

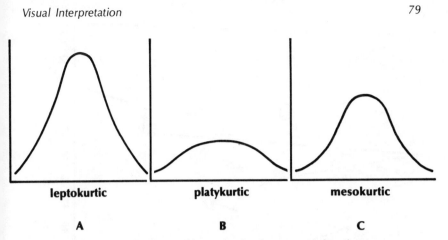

leptokurtic   platykurtic   mesokurtic

A   B   C

Figure 4.15 Three degrees of kurtosis for frequency distributions.

by a series of bars, a curve, and other geometric figures which portray changes in the value of variable quantities. Teachers use graphs in class to convey information in various subject-matter presentations. Except for very young children, graphs will not be new to students, and they should have a basic understanding of them. Most adults are familiar with bar graphs, line graphs, pictographs, pie charts, and other graphs. The histogram, frequency polygon, and cumulative frequency polygon are, for the most part, already well understood by the adult population. The graph has the advantage of providing a well-organized set of data in a form other than a set of unorganized test scores, a narrative presentation, or a table of scores.

Particularly in elementary school classes and even in classes in junior and senior high school, students may not be able to readily grasp the meaning of tabular representations of test scores. The pictorially presented data may provide the necessary vehicle to make a test score meaningful for a student. During presentations to parent groups, other faculty, or administrators, the teacher may find that a graph will be helpful to point up results of testing.

Teachers who teach more than one section of the same course can make comparisons of test performance for personal use (or other, if appropriate) by placing the two or more score distributions on the same graph as frequency polygons. Figure 4.16 illustrates how two superimposed frequency polygons look for two different classes taking the general science test. The frequency of the various scores for classes A and B can be compared by use of this graphic representation of the raw scores for both classes. Relative general performance of the two groups can be determined on the dimensions of heterogeneity, test difficulty, and overall achievement. With only the information from Figure 4.16, what comparisons would you make for the three mentioned factors?

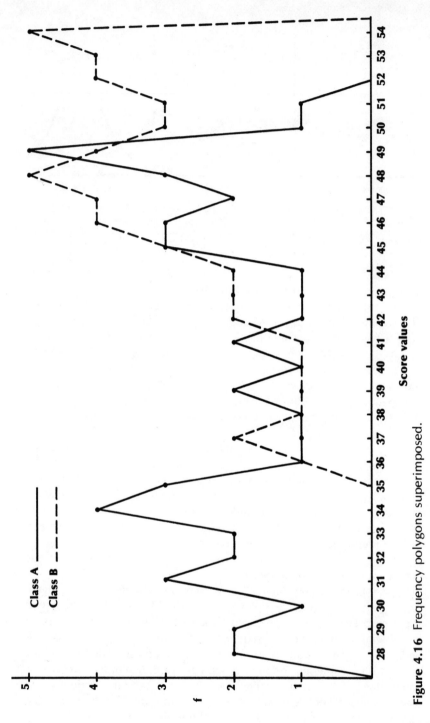

Figure 4.16 Frequency polygons superimposed.

5 Standard Score Interpretation

When the need for information from tests directs the teacher to norm-referenced score interpretation s/he must decide how to report student achievement or performance. Test scores are indexes of measurement and mean little or nothing in and of themselves; they must be given meaning in some way. Interpretation of scores by norm referencing is designed to indicate how each student compares with other students who took the same test. The teacher may compare each student with the other students in the classroom who took the test at the same time and/or with performance of one or more classes which took the same test earlier. When the teacher uses the class to interpret student performance, s/he is using an internal norming procedure. When student scores from previous classes are used, this procedure establishes an external norm group for interpreting achievement levels. High test scores are associated with high student performance, and low test scores indicate low student performance; therefore, a simple listing of the scores from the highest to the lowest provides an indication of the relative level of achievement for each student. Simple mathematical principles and procedures can be used to assist in further explanation of the scores.

Computation of standard scores (z-scores and Z-scores) allows students to use common information about all of the scores to interpret a single score from any test. Furthermore, when two or more test scores are compared or when test scores are to be combined or averaged for each student, it is not possible to use the raw scores because there is not a common unit to allow averaging of raw scores meaningfully. Since each distribution of scores has a unique mean and standard deviation, scores from separate distributions of scores are not directly comparable. Some derived score is necessary for combining test scores and making comparisons. The computation of the derived scores, z and Z, is the major topic of this chapter. The mean and standard deviation receive close attention because a thorough understanding of each is needed to comprehend what standard scores really mean. Score distributions from norm-referenced tests usually approximate the normal distribution, and the properties of the normal curve are used to interpret standard scores.

Mean

Several measures of central tendency can be obtained from a set of test scores, but the one most meaningful for our present discussion is the arithmetical average—the mean ($\overline{X}$). The mean value for a set of scores is a **representative** value for the total distribution. Each score contributes to the mean value by a weighting of the distance of the score from all other scores. The mean, when used as a measure of central tendency, is that point in a group of scores around which the scores tend to center, and it is used as the most representative value for the set. By computing the mean, the classroom teacher is able to see how each student's achievement relates to the average class performance, and the mean can be used to make comparisons of performance for two or more classes who took the same test.

The average score value expressed as a mean is computed by adding all of the scores and dividing by the number of scores which were added. For example, the mean for the five scores 51, 55, 56, 58, and 60 is computed by adding the five score values (total = 280) and dividing by 5 (N = 5). By dividing 280 by 5 (280 ÷ 5), the mean of 56 is obtained.

Expressed in words:
$$\text{Mean} = \frac{\text{sum of all scores}}{\text{number of scores}}$$

Expressed as a formula:
$$\overline{X} = \frac{X_1 + X_2 + \cdots + X_N}{N} = \frac{\Sigma X}{N} = \frac{280}{5} = 56$$

Where:
X = any test score
$\overline{X}$ = the mean
Σ = the sum of. Uppercase Greek letter sigma (Σ) means to add all X values in the distribution.
N = the number of scores in the distribution.

Using the formula, the computation of the average of 51, 55, 56, 58, and 60 is as follows:

$$\overline{X} = \frac{\Sigma X}{N}$$

$$\overline{X} = \frac{X_1 + X_2 + X_3 + X_4 + X_5}{N}$$

$$\overline{X} = \frac{51 + 55 + 56 + 58 + 60}{5}$$

$$\overline{X} = \frac{280}{5} = 56 = \text{the mean}$$

The formula just given is the raw score formula without grouping for computation. **Group formulas** are not given because hand calculators are used so widely that grouped formulas are rarely needed. Classes rarely exceed thirty students, except for large lecture classes, and even data with quite large N's can be handled easily with the automatic hand calculator. The set of raw scores given in Figure 5.1 represents scores from a general science test that have been ordered from highest to lowest to facilitate the calculation.[1]

On a sheet of paper write the set of scores and the formula for finding the mean and follow through the calculation using the guidelines from the book.[2]

Compare your response with the following:

$$\overline{X} = \frac{\Sigma X}{N} = \frac{1320}{30} = 44$$

The mean of a set of scores is like a balance point around which the scores tend to center. If the scores were all placed along a number line and each score has the same weight, the mean would act for the scores much the same as the balance point on a seesaw would balance two persons who weighed the same and were equally distant from the place where the board is hinged.

Finding the balance point for a set of test scores is much like finding positions for the seesaw on the children's playground. The major difference is in the positioning of the balance point. On the seesaw, the

---

[1]This set of data will be used to show how a classroom teacher would employ each technique in computing and interpreting the scores as they are discussed in this chapter. Directions will be given for your calculations.

[2]Throughout the chapter the reader should do the work on a sheet of paper and check against the material in the chapter for procedure and correctness.

Raw Score X	X-X̄	(X-X̄)²
60	16	256
58	14	196
57	13	169
55	11	121
53	9	81
53	9	81
52	8	64
52	8	64
49	5	25
48	4	16
46	2	4
46	2	4
45	1	1
45	1	1
43	−1	1
43	−1	1
42	−2	4
42	−2	4
42	−2	4
40	−4	16
40	−4	16
40	−4	16
39	−5	25
39	−5	25
38	−6	36
35	−9	81
32	−12	144
30	−14	196
28	−16	256
28	−16	256
1320	Totals	2164

Figure 5.1 Data for the general science test scores.

point is stationary and weights are moved to form the balance. With test scores, the scores remain stationary, but the balance point is moved so that the scores balance. Computation of the mean involves the values from each score; therefore, extreme scores affect the value of the mean greatly. If the teacher has reason to believe that some extraneous or unusual happening caused one of the scores to be extreme (much higher than the second highest score or much lower than the second lowest score), s/he may want to remove it from the distribution for calculations because it could distort the interpretation of the rest of the scores. The mean is the most widely used measure of central tendency and especially important for our study because it is used with the standard deviation to form the standard score.

Standard Deviation

Several measures of variability can be obtained from a set of test scores, but the one most meaningful for our present discussion is the standard deviation (σ). The standard deviation value for a set of scores is a measure of the variability, or spread, of the scores in the distribution. The closer the scores are, the smaller the standard deviation, and the greater the spread of scores, the larger the deviation. The mean of the distribution is used as a reference point, and a measure of dispersion from that point is calculated from the **deviations** from that point. By squaring each of the deviations ($X - \bar{X}$) and summing, the **sum of squares** is obtained (see Figure 5.1). This value forms the numerator of the standard deviation. When this value is divided by the number of scores in the distribution, the **variance** is found. The standard deviation is the square root of the variance. The procedure is better represented by the following description.

Expressed in words:

$$\text{Standard deviation} = \sqrt{\frac{\text{Sum of}\left[\left(\begin{array}{l}\text{Deviation of each} \\ \text{score from the mean}\end{array}\right)\text{Squared}\right]}{\begin{array}{c}\text{The number} \\ \text{of scores}\end{array}}}$$

Expressed as a formula:

$$\sigma = \sqrt{\frac{\Sigma(X - \bar{X})^2}{N}}$$

Where:

σ = standard deviation
Σ = means to sum
$(X - \bar{X})$ = the deviation of each score from the mean
N = number of scores

From the previous example, the mean for 51, 55, 56, 58, and 60 was found to be 56, 280 ÷ 5 = 56. To compute the standard deviation, list the scores in the distribution under a column headed X to represent the score symbol. Next, subtract the mean from each score, thus forming the deviation value $(X - \bar{X})$ for each score. Square each deviation in the column headed $(X - \bar{X})$ to give the $(X - \bar{X})^2$ column values. When the $(X - \bar{X})^2$ column is summed, the numerator value is computed. See the following:

X	X − X̄	(X = X̄)²
60	60 − 56 = +4	16
58	58 − 56 = +2	4
56	56 − 56 = 0	0
55	55 − 56 = −1	1
51	51 − 56 = −5	25
	0	46

For a graphic explanation of the above calculation, see Figure 5.2.

Substituting in the formula:

$$\sigma = \sqrt{\frac{\Sigma(X - \bar{X})^2}{N}} = \sqrt{\frac{46}{5}} = \sqrt{9.2} = 3.03$$

Compute the standard deviation from the data in Figure 5.1 by substituting in the formula before checking the computation below.

$$\sigma = \sqrt{\frac{\Sigma(X - \bar{X})^2}{N}} = \sqrt{\frac{2164}{30}} = \sqrt{72.133} = 8.49$$

The standard deviation is widely used as a measure of variability and is especially valuable to the classroom teacher who is interpreting test scores. Since the standard deviation is based on the mean value, the two computed statistics are combined into standard scores, and reports of student relative standings are reported. In the interpretation of scores from tests, some common **unit** is needed to equate differences from distribution to distribution. In the next section the mean and standard deviation are used together to build the standard score, which gives a unit for measuring in education much as the quart, liter, meter, mile and such are used in physical measurement when physical properties are of concern.

Standard Scores

When the set of raw scores was changed to deviation scores, a **transformation** was made. Some properties of the distribution were changed, but others were not. The mean value of deviation scores is

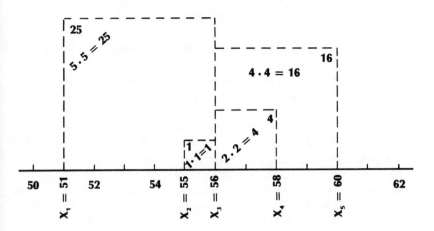

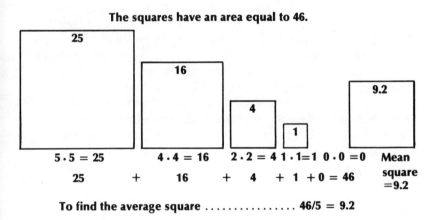

Figure 5.2 Graphic representation for mean square of 60, 58, 56, 55, and 51.

zero. The variability of a set of deviation scores is the same as it was in the original distribution. If a single deviation score is divided by the standard deviation, that deviation is transformed into standard deviation units. If a score is two standard deviation units above the mean, it becomes +2 when the deviation is divided by the standard deviation. This principle is very important in interpretation of student test scores and is used to produce a standard score that allows other transformations to be used in score interpretation.

NEED FOR STANDARD SCORES

Standard scores are needed to communicate to students and other interested persons where a score fits in relation to all other scores. If the person being reported to understands the score being reported, s/he has a ready-built interpretation system for viewing relative standings.

Another important feature of standard scores allows the teacher to make meaningful interpretations between and among scores of two or more tests. During a six-, eight-, or nine-week grading period, the classroom teacher usually has given several quizzes, a few tests, and possibly an end-of-the-term examination. Combining scores on tests of different lengths which have different means and standard deviations becomes an impossible task. It is not impossible mathematically because the numbers can be treated with the processes of mathematics. The problem arises when a meaningful value does not appear. Sometimes the way test scores are handled looks much like the addition of 5 pears, 3 apples, 6 figs, and 4 kumquats—the total of 18 is easily computed, but what does it mean? Try to get meaning from addition of 4 sheep and 6 baseballs, and you have much the same problem the teacher has when raw scores are averaged. Scores from tests which are equal in weight are directly averageable using standard scores, and those which vary in weight can be weighted and all combined to make them meaningful.

By use of standard scores, it becomes possible to determine each student's average achievement or accomplishment. Since tests have different means and standard deviations, the raw scores can not be averaged without first converting them into values with common meaning such as standard scores give. When raw scores are converted to standard scores, they become directly comparable and can be added, averaged, and combined with equal weight when the two score distributions approximate the normal distribution which has a mean of zero and a standard deviation of one. Fortunately, classroom test score distributions are usually close enough to the normal bell-shaped curve to use it as a model for score interpretation. Figure 5.3 provides a view of the normal curve and areas associated with baseline data and equivalent values for selected transformations.

A standard score can be used to express each student's score in terms of the number of standard deviation units of the score from the mean or in transformations thereof. For purposes of illustration, let us view the raw scores for Dave on two general science tests in the same class of students—first test 57 and second test 46. The two test raw scores can not be averaged meaningfully because of the different means and standard deviations for the two test distributions. The units are not com-

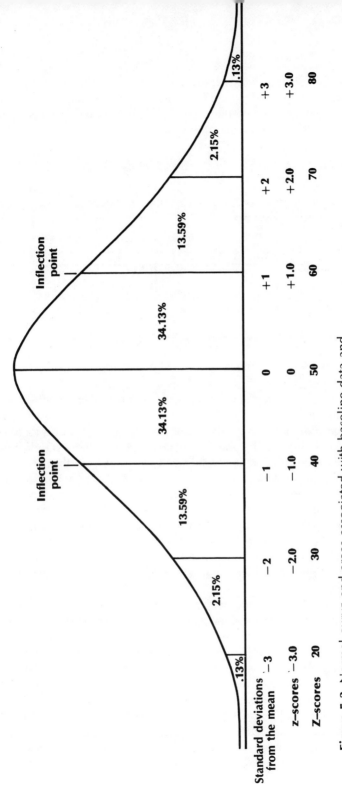

Figure 5.3 Normal curve and areas associated with baseline data and equivalent values for selected transformations.

parable for the two tests, and any raw score value would mean something entirely different if moved from one distribution to the other. The following graphical representation of the distributions show how wrong it would be to average the raw scores.

First test   Mean 50   Standard deviation 6.4

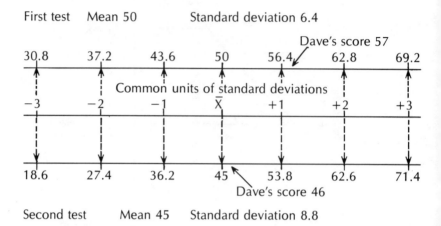

Second test   Mean 45   Standard deviation 8.8

From the graph, Dave's score of 57 on the first test appears to be about 54.3 on the second scale, and his second score of 46 appears to be about 50.8 on the first. Note the comparable scores for the first and second tests which appear at the exact points where standard deviation units fall above and below the mean. Interpreting further, Dave's score on the second test was 46 giving him a score just above the mean. Note that on the first test, a score of 46 is below the mean for the distribution. Dave's score on the first test is more than one standard deviation above the mean, but his score on the second test is close to the mean score value. Kimberly, one of Dave's classmates, scored 37 on the first test and 54 on the second test. As you can see by the graph, she improved considerably but neither the 37 nor 54 is directly related to scores in the other test's distribution scale.

To further explain the relationship, refer to the mean ($\overline{X}$) of 50 on the first test and the associated standard deviation (σ) of 6.4. The mean is a measure of the average score, and the standard deviation is the measure of the variability. To locate the points plus or minus 1, 2, or 3 standard deviations above or below the mean, the value 6.4 is added or subtracted successively to place raw-score values at the six named points. To compute the scale values for the points above, add 6.4 to 50, giving 56.4; then add 6.4 to 56.4, giving 62.8; then add 6.4 to 62.8, giving 69.2. Below the mean, subtract 6.4 successively three times and check your values with the scale given previously. To check your understanding, you should now compute the values given for the second distribution, using a mean of 45 and a standard deviation of 8.8. Compare your figures with the scale.

The values $-3, -2, -1, 0, +1, +2, +3$ are standard scores for the first-scale values of 30.8, 37.6, 43.6, 50, 56.4, 62.8, 69.2. The values $-3, -2, -1, 0, +1, +2, +3$ are standard scores for the second-scale values of 18.6, 27.4, 36.2, 45, 53.8, 62.6, 71.4. The lowest score value of 30.8 on scale one is equivalent to a score of 18.6 on the second scale. The same relationship holds for all points located at comparable points on the scales. Interpretations could be estimated between scales, as was done before; however, a transformation allows more accuracy than can be obtained through the graphic representation. The scale -3, $-2, -1, 0, +1, +2, +3$ provides a common scale for interpretation between the two raw score distribution scales, and for averaging scores from one or more tests. The next section shows how the transformation is made by using the measure of the mean and the measure of the standard deviation.

z-SCORES

Raw scores can be made comparable by expressing them in the same size units based on a new distribution which has a mean of zero and a standard deviation of one. By subtracting the mean from each raw score and dividing by the standard deviation, a z-score is obtained for each score. If the new distribution of values were added and divided by N, the mean would be zero. The new standard deviation would be one. Each z-score indicates the number of standard deviation units an individual score is from the mean of the distribution—either the original mean or the mean of the z-score distribution.

The formula for this linear transformation is:

Expressed in words:

$$\text{Standard score} = \frac{\text{raw score} - \text{the mean}}{\text{standard deviation}}$$

Expressed as a formula:

$$z = \frac{X - \bar{X}}{\sigma}$$

Where:

z = a standard score
X = any raw score
$\bar{X}$ = the mean
σ = the standard deviation

Substituting for Dave's raw score on the first general science test X in the formula, a more accurate value can be found on the middle scale:

$$z = \frac{X - \bar{X}}{\sigma} = \frac{57 - 50}{6.4} = \frac{7}{6.4} = +1.09.$$

Substituting for Dave's raw score on the second general science test for X, in the formula, the value on the middle scale is:

$$z = \frac{X - \bar{X}}{\sigma} = \frac{46 - 45}{8.8} = \frac{1}{8.8} = +.11.$$

Comparisons can now be made between the two standard scores, and the scores can be averaged. Graphically, Dave's two scores based on the transformations of deviations in units of the standard deviations look like this:

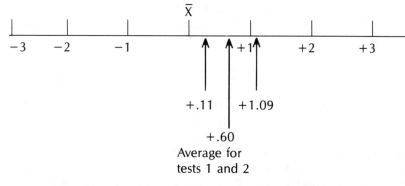

+.60
Average for
tests 1 and 2

Dave's achievement or performance within the class was better on the first test than the second test, although both test scores were above the average (mean) for the class. The average for both scores (+.60) illustrates that by changing the raw scores to standard scores, the unit is defined so it means the same to everyone. The z-score unit, defined as one standard deviation unit, becomes a standard measure much like other standard units used in physical measurement. The z-score values are reported to the nearest hundredth of a unit. The one-unit range from the mean to the point one standard deviation above the mean serves as an example for the other scale units and looks like this:

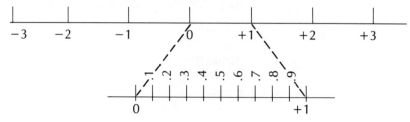

Viewing and comparing the graphical representations of the first and second general science test scores, one can see that the two raw test scores of 57 and 46 could not be averaged since they are not based on the same score units. The graphical representation of Dave's two scores on the linear transformation shows how the scores are comparable when transformed into standard-score units.

The use of standard scores means that the standard deviation is being used as the unit of measurement. In the preceding examples, Dave's score of 57 ($z = +1.09$) on the first test is 1.09 standard deviation units above the mean, while Kimberly's score of 37 ($z = -2.03$) on the first test is 2.03 standard deviation units below the mean. The z-score distribution is widely used in statistical procedures, but our discussion will be limited to its use to glean meaning from test scores.

As shown in previous examples, z-scores require a sign to indicate the direction of the score from the mean, positive if above and negative if below. When recording, calculating, or reporting z-scores, it is easy to drop a sign or in some way to change a value from negative to positive or vice versa. In addition, the decimals may make utilization of z-scores cumbersome for some persons or situations. The small range of scores, typically about six standard deviation units (roughly from -3.00 to $+3.00$), and a very small standard deviation may make differences among scores difficult to interpret. A transformation to another score, the Z-score is available to overcome the difficulties associated with use of z-scores when reporting test performance.

Z-SCORES

A new set of scores (Z-scores) which retain the original relationship but avoids the difficulties stated above can be found by the following transformation:

Expressed in words:

Z equals ten times the z-score plus fifty.

Expressed as a formula:

$$Z = 10(z) + 50$$

Where:

Z = standard score with a mean of 50 and a standard deviation of 10

z = original standard score

10 = a constant which sets the value of the new standard deviation

50 = a constant which sets the value of the new mean

The formula for Z may also be rewritten as follows:

$$Z = 10 \left[\frac{X - \bar{X}}{\sigma} \right] + 50$$

Where:

Z = standard score with a mean of 50 and a standard deviation of 10

$$\frac{X - \bar{X}}{\sigma} = \text{a z-score}$$

Other standard score distributions can be created by varying the two constants in the basic Z-score formula ($Z = 10z + 50$). If a z-score is multiplied by 100, the standard deviation becomes 100. If 500 is added, the new mean is 500. These transformations form a distribution which has a mean of 500 and a standard deviation of 100. This distribution is widely used to report performance on standardized tests. Figure 5.4 shows some standard scores used to report test results from standardized tests.

$$z = 1(\sigma) + 0$$
transformed to
CEEB = 100(z) + 500
AGCT = 20(z) + 100
Deviation IQs
Wechsler = 15(z) + 100
Stanford-Binet = 16(z) + 100

Figure 5.4 Standard scores used to report results from standardized tests.

The general formula for obtaining a standard score distribution with a new mean and new standard deviation from a raw score distribution is as follows:

Expressed in words:

Transformed Standard Score = $\begin{bmatrix} \text{New} \\ \text{standard} \\ \text{deviation} \end{bmatrix} \begin{bmatrix} \text{Score} - \dfrac{\text{Mean of the raw}}{\text{score distribution}} \\ \hline \text{Standard deviation of the} \\ \text{raw score distribution} \end{bmatrix} + \begin{matrix} \text{New} \\ \text{mean} \end{matrix}$

Expressed as a formula:

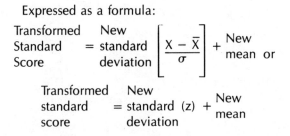

$$\text{Transformed Standard Score} = \text{New standard deviation} \left[\frac{X - \bar{X}}{\sigma} \right] + \text{New mean} \quad \text{or}$$

$$\text{Transformed standard score} = \text{New standard deviation} \ (z) + \text{New mean}$$

From Figure 5.1 four raw scores are selected to illustrate the calculation of a transformed standard score (Z):

$$Z_{40} = 10 \frac{X - \bar{X}}{\sigma} + 50 \qquad\qquad Z_{60} = 10 \frac{X - \bar{X}}{\sigma} + 50$$

$$Z_{40} = 10 \frac{40 - 44}{8.49} + 50 \qquad\qquad Z_{60} = 10 \frac{60 - 44}{8.49} + 50$$

$$Z_{40} = 10 \frac{-4}{8.49} + 50 \qquad\qquad Z_{60} = 10 \frac{16}{8.49} + 50$$

$$Z_{40} = (10)(-.47) + 50 \qquad\qquad Z_{60} = (10)(1.88) + 50$$

$$Z_{40} = -4.7 + 50 \qquad\qquad Z_{60} = 18.8 + 50$$

$$Z_{40} = 45.3 \cong 45 \qquad\qquad Z_{60} = 68.8 \cong 69$$

$$Z_{28} = 10 \frac{X - \bar{X}}{\sigma} + 50 \qquad\qquad Z_{48} = 10 \frac{X - \bar{X}}{\sigma} + 50$$

$$Z_{28} = 10 \frac{28 - 44}{8.49} + 50 \qquad\qquad Z_{48} = 10 \frac{48 - 44}{8.49} + 50$$

$$Z_{28} = 10 \frac{-16}{8.49} + 50 \qquad\qquad Z_{48} = 10 \frac{4}{8.49} + 50$$

$$Z_{28} = (10)(-1.88) + 50 \qquad\qquad Z_{48} = (10)(.47) + 50$$

$$Z_{28} = -18.8 + 50 \qquad\qquad Z_{48} = 4.7 + 50$$

$$Z_{28} = 31.2 \cong 31 \qquad\qquad Z_{48} = 54.7 \cong 55$$

The Z-score transformation increases the standard deviation to 10 units and the mean to 50. Pictorially the distribution looks like this:

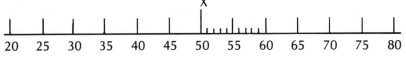

20 25 30 35 40 45 50 55 60 65 70 75 80

Using Dave's two z-scores, the transformation looks like this:

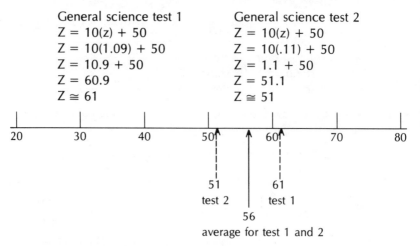

General science test 1
$Z = 10(z) + 50$
$Z = 10(1.09) + 50$
$Z = 10.9 + 50$
$Z = 60.9$
$Z \cong 61$

General science test 2
$Z = 10(z) + 50$
$Z = 10(.11) + 50$
$Z = 1.1 + 50$
$Z = 51.1$
$Z \cong 51$

51
test 2

61
test 1

56
average for test 1 and 2

The first general science Z-score was 61, the second general science Z-score was 51, and these scores are averageable (56 average) because the Z-score distribution has the same properties as the z-score distribution with the exceptions of mean and standard deviation values.

USING NORMAL CURVE CHARACTERISTICS

The discussion in this chapter has been concerned with the mean, standard deviation, and standard scores (z-score and Z-score). Each of these characteristics can be related to the bell-shaped curve known as the normal curve or normal probability distribution. The graphical representation of the normal curve in Figure 5.3 presents an opportunity for further visual interpretation and study of the properties of the normal curve, which can be used to aid in interpretation of a set of test scores, to compare performances of one individual in different testing situations, and to compare a student's score to the performance of another group of students on the same test.

A measure of central tendency (the mean) and a measure of variability (the standard deviation) have been used to transform the obtained score into the standard z-score and the standard Z-score. The z-score is expressed in standard units from the unit normal distribution and is interpreted by properties of the normal curve. The normal distribution can be considered to be made up of a family of an infinite number of possible distributions depending on central location and variability. In-

z-score (standard deviations from the mean)	Z-score	Percent of area under the curve below the point (approximate)
+3.0	80	100
+2.5	75	99
+2.0	70	97
+1.5	65	93
+1.0	60	84
+0.5	55	69
−0.0	50	50
−0.5	45	31
−1.0	40	16
−1.5	35	7
−2.0	30	3
−2.5	25	1
−3.0	20	0

Figure 5.5 Areas for chosen segments of the baseline under the curve corresponding to standard deviations and Z-scores.

terpretation of z-scores uses the unit normal curve where the mean is 0 and the standard deviation is 1.

The basic z-score is a standard score from which other linear standard scores such as the Z-score may be computed. The z-score and Z-score differ only in units used to express the means and standard deviations. If, for example, Daniel had a z-score of 1 or a Z-score of 60, either score, 1 or 60, is 1.0 standard deviation above the mean, which indicates that he did as well or better than 84 percent of the group taking the test. The 84 percent was determined by adding all percentages below the standard score +1.00 or a 60 Z-score (34.13 + 34.13 + 13.59 + 2.15 + .13). A percent may be determined relative to any standard score using knowledge about the normal curve. For example, a student achieving a 55 Z-score did as well as or better than about 69 percent of the group taking the test. The 69 percent was determined by adding all percentages below the standard point of .5 or a 55 Z-score (19.15 + 34.14 + 13.59 + 2.15 + .13). Figure 5.5 presents standard deviations, corresponding to Z-score values, and the percent under chosen areas of the baseline of the curve corresponding to these points. A table for the more exact measurement of areas of the normal curve in terms of z-score as well as additional discussion can be found in *Describing Data Statistically.*[3] Areas of the

---

[3] Charles D. Hopkins, *Describing Data Statistically* (Columbus, Ohio: Charles E. Merrill Publishing Company, 1974), pp. 75–81, 114–16.

curve for segments of the baseline of the curve may be computed for the normal curve following the instructions in the reference provided. When interpreting scores from tests, frequencies of occurrence on the baseline and percentages are likened to values for the normal distribution. The area under the curve being equal to N, the frequencies are interpreted according to normal distribution values.

6 Other Relationships

Within a distribution of scores and the interval established by the lowest score and the highest score, many points can be used to explain relationships among scores. The raw scores can be converted to derived scores, which make it possible to compare scores from different tests by expressing them in the same unit of measurement. This also helps in interpreting test scores to students, parents, educators, and other interested persons. The procedures to be discussed in this chapter help to explain further the relationship of a score to other scores in the distribution by using knowledge of the rank order and other ways to interpret individual performance relative to the performance of other individuals within a group.

In many situations it is important to know how a particular score compares with scores made by students in other classes in the same school or school system, schools in other parts of the country, and in other particular situations. A test score or scores can be compared through different systems of reporting norms. Percentiles, percentile ranks, stanines, and other types of derived norms provide ways to show relationships among scores obtained from students in a classroom and an external norm group.

Percentiles

A percentile is one of ninety-nine points that divide an ordered distribution of scores into one hundred equal parts. Each percentile shows the place in the distribution where a designated proportion of the total distribution falls below it. For example, P_{50} is a score value where 50 percent of the scores are less than the P_{50} score value.

A student's score can be compared with percentile points to

help locate it in the distribution of scores. For example, a score could be reported to be less than the P_{50} value, or between P_{45} and P_{50}. Percentile points can also be used to report a comparison of classroom scores to some other group. Computation can be performed to determine a point below which any percent of the scores will lie. The general formula for finding percentile points is:

$$P_p = L + \left[\frac{pN - f_b}{f_n} \right] i$$

Where:

P_p = any one of the 99 percentile points

L = the exact lower limit of the interval which contains P_p

N = the total number of scores

p = the proportion of scores falling below the point

f_b = the number of scores falling below L

f_n = the number of scores in the interval which contains P_p

i = The interval size (Computation for most classroom tests uses ungrouped data; therefore, the interval is one and drops out of computation.)

Expressed in words:

$$P_p = \begin{array}{c} \text{Exact lower} \\ \text{limit of the} \\ \text{interval} \\ \text{which} \\ \text{contains } P_p \end{array} + \left[\frac{\begin{array}{c} \text{(the proportion} \quad \text{number of} \\ \text{of scores below} \quad \text{scores falling} \\ \text{the point) times} \;-\; \text{below the inter-} \\ \text{(total number of} \quad \text{val which con-} \\ \text{scores)} \qquad\qquad \text{tains } P_p \end{array}}{\begin{array}{c} \text{the number of scores in the} \\ \text{interval which contains } P_p \end{array}} \right] \begin{array}{c} \text{Width} \\ \text{of the} \\ \text{class} \\ \text{interval} \end{array}$$

Using the general science test scores in Figure 4.4 in Chapter 4, the 25th percentile (P_{25}) is computed as follows:

$$P_p = L + \left(\frac{pN - f_b}{f_n} \right) i$$

$$P_{25} = 38.5 + \left(\frac{7.5 - 6}{5} \right) (3)$$

$$P_{25} = 38.5 + \left(\frac{1.5}{5} \right) \left(\frac{3}{1} \right)$$

$$P_{25} = 38.5 + \frac{4.5}{5}$$

$$P_{25} = 38.5 + .9 = 39.4$$

The twenty-fifth percentile (P_{25} = 39.4) is the point below which exactly 25 percent of the distribution of scores falls. Computation of the seventy-fifth percentile (P_{75}) for the same distribution of scores is as follows:

$$P_{75} = 50.5 + \left[\frac{22.5 - 22}{4}\right] 3$$

$$P_{75} = 50.5 + \left(\frac{.5}{4}\right)\left(\frac{3}{1}\right)$$

$$P_{75} = 50.5 + \frac{1.5}{4}$$

$$P_{75} = 50.5 + .37 = 50.87$$

The seventy-fifth percentile (P_{75} = 50.87) is the point below which exactly 75 percent of the distribution of scores falls.

UNGROUPED DATA COMPUTATION

Computation of percentile equivalents for ungrouped (interval of one) raw scores requires a listing of the raw scores in decreasing magnitude. A cumulative frequency column is needed to locate percentile points. Figure 6.1 provides the raw scores, frequency, and cumulative frequency for the general science test. Computations of P_{25} and P_{75} with ungrouped data are:

$$P_p = L + \left[\frac{pN - f_b}{f_n}\right] 1$$

$$P_{25} = 38.5 + \left[\frac{7.5 - 6}{2}\right] 1 \qquad P_{75} = 51.5 + \left[\frac{22.5 - 22}{2}\right] 1$$

$$P_{25} = 38.5 + \frac{1.5}{2} \qquad P_{75} = 51.5 + \frac{.5}{2}$$

$$P_{25} = 38.5 + .75 = 39.25 \qquad P_{75} = 51.5 + .25 = 51.75$$

OTHER NAMES FOR PERCENTILE POINTS

In professional literature, standardized test manuals, and school reports, reference is often made to points in the distribution in terms other than percentiles. In general, each of these points will be a percentile. Median, quartile, and decile are briefly denoted in the next sections.

Median

The point which is halfway through a distribution of scores (P_{50}) is also called the median. This point is used as a measure of central

Raw Score X	Frequency f	Cumulative Frequency cf
60	1	30
58	1	29
57	1	28
55	1	27
53	2	26
52	2	24
49	1	22
48	1	21
46	2	20
45	2	18
43	2	16
42	3	14
40	3	11
39	2	8
38	1	6
35	1	5
32	1	4
30	1	3
28	2	2

Figure 6.1 Raw scores for the general science test.

tendency when the data are ordered. The median is also used as a measure of score concentration if a distribution of scores has one or a few extreme scores which could weight the mean too heavily and distort the mean measure.

Heavily skewed distributions can be identified by comparing the two measures—the mean and the median. For heavy positive skewness, the mean will be above (greater than) the median. For heavy negative skewness, the mean will be below (less than) the median.

Quartile

A quartile (P_{25}, P_{50}, P_{75}) is one of three points which divide an ordered distribution of scores into four equal parts. Q_1 (P_{25}) is one-fourth of the way through the distribution, Q_2 (P_{50}, median) is one-half of the way through, and Q_3 (P_{75}) is three-fourths of the way through. These points can be used to establish intervals for discussion of obtained scores to external distributions of scores. For example, when comparing classroom test scores on a standardized test, the teacher could group the scores for students in a class in fourths according to manual norms. Statements could be made about how many in the class had scores in each of the intervals established by the quartiles. The set of scores could be reviewed as follows: in the fifth grade one-third of the students' scores were above Q_3, nearly two-thirds between Q_2 and Q_3, and only one-tenth of the students' scores fell below Q_2. In the norm group, one-fourth of the scores would be in each range; therefore, this class performed at a higher level than the norm group.

Decile

A decile (P_{10}, P_{20}, ... P_{90}) is one of nine points that divide an ordered distribution of scores into ten equal parts. D_1 (P_{10}) is one-tenth of the way through the distribution, D_2 (P_{20}) is two-tenths, and so on. The points are used to divide the distribution much the same way as quartiles when smaller intervals are needed for reporting student performance.

Percentile Rank

The percentile rank indicates the percentage of all the scores in a distribution that fall below a given raw score. Percentile ranks are computed by arranging the raw scores in descending magnitude and finding the number of scores equal to or falling below a given score and reporting those equal to or falling below as a percentage of the total. Percentile ranks (PR) can be computed by using the following formula:

$$PR = \left(\frac{100}{N}\right)\left(f_b + \left[\frac{(X - L)\,(f_n)}{i}\right]\right)$$

Where:

PR = percentile rank
X = score whose percentile rank is desired
N = number of scores in the distribution
f_b = cumulative frequency up to the class interval containing X
L = lower real limit of the class interval containing X
f_n = frequency in the class containing X
i = the class interval (If equal to 1, this drops out of the computation.)

Expressed in words:

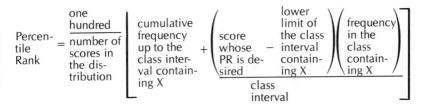

Using the data from Figure 4.3, the teacher can find the percentile rank for the raw score of 52 by substitution in the following formula. The computation follows:

$$PR = \frac{100}{N} \left[f_b + \frac{(X - L) f_n}{i} \right]$$

$$PR_{52} = \frac{100}{30} \left[22 + \frac{(52 - 51.5)2}{1} \right]$$

$$PR_{52} = 3.33 \left[22 + (.5)(2) \right]$$

$$PR_{52} = (3.33)(22 + 1)$$

$$PR_{52} = (3.33)(23) = 76.59 \cong 77$$

Percentile rank can be used to establish percentile rank norms for a class, but more important for our study, standardized tests usually report norms in terms of the percentile rank for raw scores. Interpretation of the percentage of students falling below a given score is easy for students and parents to understand. A percentile rank is straightforward in reporting the percent of the group a particular score exceeds and allows a single score on the test to be compared to the test table of percentile rank norms. The percentile rank of a score may be appoximated from a curve such as the one in Figure 4.10. The cumulative-frequency polygon is accompanied by a scale for reading percentile ranks. By reading directly from a baseline value to the line of the graph and across to the percentile rank scale, the reader can make a very close estimate of the percentile rank. Figure 6.2 gives a more direct reading of relationships among the raw score distribution, the percentile scale, and the percentile rank scale. The percentile rank may also be determined exactly through computation as discussed.

Figure 6.2 also points up the basic difference between a percentile and a percentile rank. If the question is asked about what percent of the scores fall below a specific score value, then the answer is a percentile rank, but if the question is asked about what score divides the distribution at a specific percentage of the scores, then the answer is a percentile. In the first case, the answer is a percentage of the scores (PR), and in the second case the answer is a score value (P).

PERCENTILE BANDS

Some test publishers have begun to use percentile rank bands. The percentile rank band is a range of percentile ranks or a raw score range that is expected to include the student's true score at a given probability level. Percentile rank bands take into consideration the inaccuracy of measurement in making comparisons. The bands emphasize that test-measurement error is present in each score. They discourage the

Percentiles	Raw Score	Percentile Rank
	61 <	100
	60 <	98
	58 <	95
	57 <	92
$P_{90} = 55.5$ ---->		
	55 <	88
	53 <	85
$P_{80} = 52$ ---->	52 <	80
	49 <	73
$P_{70} = 48.5$ ---->		
	48 <	68
	46 <	63
$P_{60} = 45.5$ ---->		
	45 <	57
$P_{50} = 43$ ---->	43 <	50
	42 <	42
$P_{40} = 41.83$ ---->		
$P_{30} = 39.83$ ---->	40 <	32
	39 <	23
$P_{20} = 38.5$ ---->		
	38 <	18
	35 <	15
	32 <	12
$P_{10} = 30.5$ ---->	30 <	8
	28 <	3
	27 <	0

Figure 6.2 Relationships between raw scores, percentiles, and percentile ranks for the raw scores of the general science test.

test user from attaching too much precision to a test score. The reported band usually extends one standard error of measurement on either side of the obtained score, giving a **confidence interval** of 68 percent for that band.

When percentile bands for scores overlap, the difference in achievement is not significant. If percentile bands do not overlap, then the differences in achievement are significant. Classroom teachers can make percentile bands from percentile ranks and the standard error of measurement for their classroom tests. Figure 6.3 illustrates how percentile rank bands may be used.

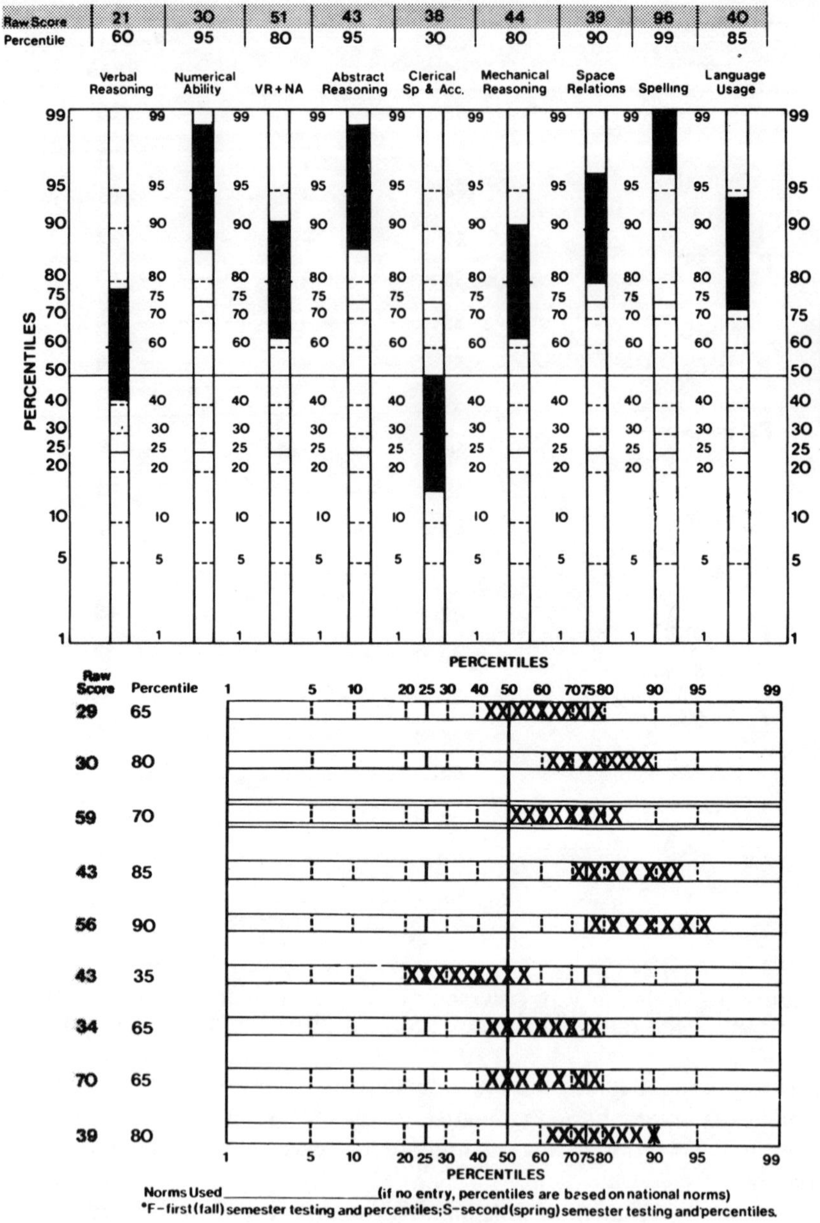

Figure 6.3 Two ways to present percentile rank bands
SOURCE: Charles Hopkins and Richard Antes, *Classroom Measurement and Evaluation* (Itasca, Ill.: F. E. Peacock, 1978), p. 385.

Stanines

Stanine, which is short for standard nine, is a normally distributed standard score which has values from 1 through 9. Stanines do not represent specific points on a scale of scores but bands of scores, with a middle band having limits established by points above and below the mean. Stanines are determined by dividing the distribution of scores into groups based on intervals of one-half of a standard deviation. Each stanine except 1 and 9 is one-half of a standard deviation in width, with the middle stanine of 5 extending from one-quarter standard deviation below the mean to one-quarter standard deviation above the mean. A normal distribution of stanine scores has a mean of 5 and a standard deviation of approximately 2. Figure 6.4 shows the percentage for each stanine in a normally distributed set of scores, deviations, and stanine numbers. Figure 6.5 is the stanine scale showing rounded percents on each score from 1 to 9. The rounded percents will be utilized in computing stanines.

Figures 6.4 and 6.5 show the assigned percentage for each stanine. For assignment of stanines for the general science test scores in Figure 6.1, the rounded percentages shown in Figure 6.5 are used. The steps in computing stanines are as follows:

1. Set up a frequency distribution as in Figure 6.6, and record in the frequency column the number of students obtaining each score.
2. Find the cumulative frequency for each test score.
3. The cumulative frequencies are changed to percentages by multiplying every cumulative frequency value by 100/N.
4. The cumulative percent for the stanines is used to assign stanine values starting from the bottom of the cumulative percentages for each score using the following percentages for each stanine.

Cumulative percentages	0 to 4	5 to 11	12 to 23	24 to 40	41 to 60	61 to 77	78 to 89	90 to 96	97 to 100
for the stanine scale									
Stanine assignment	1	2	3	4	5	6	7	8	9

In the fourth column of Figure 6.6 (cumulative percentages) for the raw score of 28, the cumulative percentage is seen to be 7. Since 4 percent of the stanines should be ones, and 7 percent of the scores are scores of 28, the two scores of 28 get a stanine equivalent of 1. Eleven percent of the scores fall in stanine 2 or below, thus scores of 29 and 30 receive a stanine equivalent of 2. The cumulative percentage for each stanine range is compared to the actual cumulative percentages of the distribution of raw scores as was done for stanines 1 and 2, using the values from step 4 above. Given a set of scores with a large N and

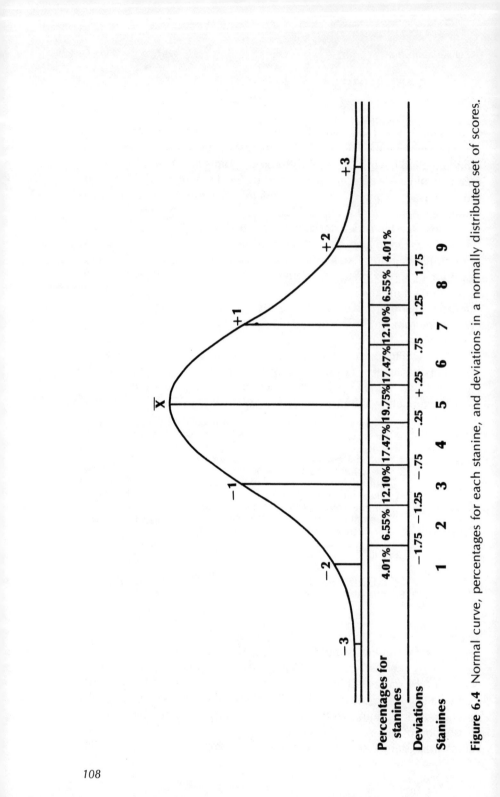

Figure 6.4 Normal curve, percentages for each stanine, and deviations in a normally distributed set of scores.

Percentages for stanines	4.01%	6.55%	12.10%	17.47%	19.75%	17.47%	12.10%	6.55%	4.01%
Deviations	−1.75	−1.25	−.75	−.25	+.25	.75	1.25	1.75	
Stanines	1	2	3	4	5	6	7	8	9

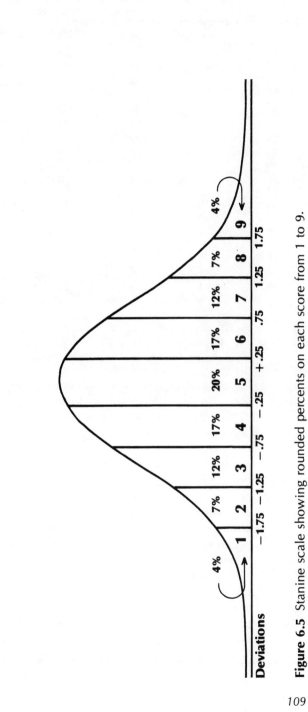

Figure 6.5 Stanine scale showing rounded percents on each score from 1 to 9.

Raw Score X	Frequency f	Cumulative Frequency cf	Cumulative Percentage (cf)(100/N)	Stanine	Stanine Frequency
60	1	30	100	9	
58	1	29	97	9	2
57	1	28	93	8	
55	1	27	90	8	2
53	2	26	87	7	
52	2	24	80	7	4
49	1	22	73	6	
48	1	21	70	6	
46	2	20	67	6	4
45	2	18	60	5	
43	2	16	53	5	7
42	3	14	47	5	
40	3	11	37	4	
39	2	8	27	4	5
38	1	6	20	3	
35	1	5	17	3	3
32	1	4	13	3	
30	1	3	10	2	1
28	2	2	7	1	2
Totals	30				30

Figure 6.6 Assignment of stanines to a set of general science test scores according to the four-step procedure.

measurement on a trait which is normally distributed, the stanines approach a normal distribution. With small numbers in a distribution, a teacher should expect to have some differences from a perfectly symmetrical distribution.

A stanine table[1] showing the number of students to be assigned to each stanine for groups containing 20 to 100 cases is available and allows direct assignment from an ordering of the scores. By use of a table, stanines can be easily assigned to test results. Figure 6.7 gives the values for stanines for different sizes (N) of distributions. If classes are larger than thirty-five, the table can easily be extended by using the percentages expected for each of the 9 stanines. The table can be used to make the assignment of stanines for classroom tests. If a table is used, all students who make the same score must receive the same stanine equivalent. Violation of this rule to assure a symmetrical distribution would be unfair if a score for one student is placed in stanine 7 and the same score value for another student is placed in stanine 8 to fit the chart. It is better to

[1] W. N. Durost, *The Characteristics, Use, and Computation of Stanines* (New York: Harcourt, Brace, Jovanovich, Inc., 1961).

violate the neat distribution than to make an arbitrary decision which could affect a student's record and future rapport between student and teacher.

Number in group	Number in each stanine								
35	1	3	4	6	7	6	4	3	1
30	1	2	4	5	6	5	4	2	1
25	1	2	3	4	5	4	3	2	1
20	1	1	2	4	4	4	2	1	1
15	1	1	2	2	3	2	2	1	1
Stanine	1	2	3	4	5	6	7	8	9

Figure 6.7 Number of scores in stanines for selected size groups.

Reporting performance in stanines rather than specific points is advantageous because it allows the use of general categories for score interpretation. The interpretation is in a broader reference, which facilitates reporting scores to students and parents. For example, stanines 1, 2, and 3 may be verbally interpreted as the lowest, lower, and low groups; stanines 4, 5, and 6 as low-average, average, and high-average groups; and stanines 7, 8, and 9 as the high, higher, and highest groups. Norms for many standardized tests are available in stanines, and the score reporting is more meaningful to some students and parents.

7 Criterion-Referenced Interpretation

The descriptive expression "criterion referenced" is a mid-sixties addition to the set of technical words used in educational measurement and evaluation. Criterion referenced is presently used to identify a system of interpreting test scores. The central idea behind criterion referencing is to use some clearly defined set of standards as a sounding board to interpret test scores, or rather test performance since test scores as such may or may not be used. Although the term is somewhat new, what it stands for is not. The principle of interpreting student performance to a set of absolute standards external to the student dates back to the earliest judgments made by teachers about students.

For centuries, teachers used a set of standards, probably a mental set rather than a written set, as a guide to judge how well a student was learning. This manner of assessment predated the formal learning center as it is now known, but it carried over into the teaching done in early American classrooms. In the early days of educational testing in America, from about 1840 to 1915, teachers continued to set their own standards for satisfactory performance without much consideration about how students could be expected to learn and to perform. If students could not learn enough to meet standards, they were considered to be slow, lazy, or—even worse—dumb.

In the mid-teens of this century (1914-17), the theory of **psychological measurement** began to include an element suggesting that some behavioral expectations based on age, level of maturity, and other student characteristics might contribute to human functioning. Psychologists suggested that, given a set of certain characteristics, there must be some average level which could be established as expected attainment. Although that average was not intended to be a standard for everyone, the average performance became a point of reference for interpretation of human behavior. The concept of average human behavior was incorporated into test interpretation when psychologists were (and still are) trying to decide what is normal behavior for each of the many different modalities. The best way to do this seemed to be to find out how a certain **sample** of the human population behaved on each psychological characteristic. This concept concerning the characteristic of sanity-insanity has been considered. It has been pointed out, that the level of sanity below which a human being could be considered as insane was relative to behavior and that if there were only one person on earth, that there could not be human behavior considered to be at the level of insanity. The behavior of that single person is normal behavior no matter what the behavior is and implies that insanity can not be dealt with in terms of absolute standards.

The early efforts to establish normed levels of behavior were thrust toward measurement of psychological traits but was later picked up in educational measurement for the testing of achievement. Soon the idea of norming for tests became the accepted practice for most standardized achievement tests used in the school setting and also in a large portion of teacher-made tests (see Chapter 8). Performance on achievement tests for a set of students was used to indicate how well a single student had performed while taking the test.

Today most persons who write about criterion-referenced tests refer to comparison of a score to a norm or norm schedule as the traditional way of interpreting scores on tests. Although it is not entirely correct to imply that norm referencing came before criterion referencing, it does reflect a change in testing practices where now some tests are interpreted one way and others in another way. With limitations, a criterion-referenced test can be used for norm-referenced measurement, and conceivably when items on a norm-referenced test can be matched to objectives, criterion-referenced interpretation can be made to scores from a test intended to be norm referenced. An overview of the implied questions is given in the following summary:

> In summary, a norm-referenced test can be used to make criterion-referenced measurements, and a criterion-referenced test can be used to make norm-referenced measurements, but neither use will be particularly satisfactory.[1]

[1] Ronald K. Hambleton, et al. "Criterion-Referenced Testing and Measurement: A Review of Technical Issues and Developments." *Review of Educational Research,* Winter, 1978, 48(1), p. 3.

Some commercial tests are considered by the publishers to be interpretable by either norm- or criterion-referencing, but the methods they use to interpret scores lose the spirit of either one or both of the two reference systems. Criterion-referencing today means more than establishing a cutoff point for satisfactory performance. The test must measure a clearly defined domain of behavior.

Some testing specialists today champion the strengths of criterion referencing while others side with norm referencing. The authors are not taking a middle-of-the-road position, but hopefully Chapters 7 and 8 will point up the strengths of each and show the reader how educators can use both forms of interpretation within a fully developed test program with each one doing what it does best. Most classroom teachers will need to build a component of each system of reference into the classroom testing program. For this chapter the attention will be given to interpretation of performance when mastery of a body of content or particular skills is needed or when a specific set of objectives which have been set in terms of clearly observable behavior in a limited range of subject-matter or skills is to serve as criterion for interpretation. Effective teaching in a school program directed to mastery learning will cause scores on criterion-referenced tests to cluster at the very upper end of the raw-score continuum **range.** This happens because criterion-referenced tests require students to do only what everyone is expected to do. Many tests are of this kind.

Objectives as Referents

In the strictest sense, all tests are written with objectives in mind. It seems inconceivable that anyone would try to build an educational measuring instrument without knowing what it is supposed to measure. All tests are based on objectives even though they are not stated or are set forth in general terms. With criterion-referenced test interpretation, a direct relationship is established between a specific objective and a series of items on the test that relate to that objective. The movement to individualized instruction, need for mastery for certain bodies of subject matter, and a thrust by some educators to apply mastery teaching with the expectation of mastery learning for all instruction have required score interpretation to behavioral objectives for certain tests. Behavioral objectives deal with specific, discrete, and measurable ends. They are concerned with particular, observable, measurable student behavior, and they establish a minimum level of acceptable performance within the objective statement.

When each specific objective describes what is to be learned, the teacher knows exactly what the instruction is to produce, and s/he can better plan for it. Thus, it becomes easier to determine the degree of student success in reaching each objective if it is presented in terms of observable behavior. Conditions which are right for use of behavioral objectives also lend themselves to criterion referencing. By using the objectives as referents, the teacher can write test items that directly measure each behavioral objective by allowing comparison of test results on a set of specific tasks to the minimum acceptance level for that objective. This is the principle used in building criterion-referenced tests, those tests whose measures will be interpreted by comparison to an absolute standard set before the testing session and before results of student test performance are known.

Mastery Testing

Those who advocate the use of criterion referencing for classroom tests point up that norm-referenced tests generate test results (scores) that are good for making decisions about groups but lack information that guides decisions about individuals. Within the classroom, teachers are occupied with students as individuals, even though much teaching may be done by group instruction. Norm-referenced tests deal with relative position but do not supply data about what students as individuals are able to do in absolute terms. Mastery of certain prerequisites and requisites makes up the basis for some classroom instruction, and mastery is necessary to indicate satisfactory learning of certain knowledge, concepts, and skills. If teaching has been to mastery, then testing must be directed the same way.

TEACHING FOR MASTERY

Certain educators propose that all classroom instruction should center on learning for mastery.[2] This movement views traditional education as serving a selective function; whereas today, many educators believe that the primary function should be the development of the individual. The humanist, the traditionalist, the progressive, and the conservative all have the same basic desire to prepare each student to live in a modern world, but philosophical orientations affect preparation of students by different groups, and teaching takes different directions. Different instruction usually requires different measurement procedures,

[2] Benjamin S. Bloom, J. Thomas Hastings, and George F. Madaus, *Handbook on Formative and Summative Evaluation of Student Learning* (New York: McGraw-Hill Book Company, 1971), pp. 43-57.

and those who advocate mastery teaching find a need for test interpretation to carefully set criterion points for a test over a well-described domain of behavior.

Closely related to the move for mastery teaching techniques or learning for mastery is the use of criterion-referenced tests and interpretation of test scores to a criterion point. The central premise for mastery learning is found in the following statement:

> Most students (perhaps more than 90 percent) can master what we have to teach them, and it is the task of instruction to find the means which will enable them to master the subject under consideration. A basic task is to determine what we mean by "mastery of the subject" and to search for the methods and materials which will enable the largest proportion of our students to attain such mastery.[3]

It could be added that the task of measurement is to find the means whereby the teacher and student will know when mastery has been achieved or, if mastery has not been achieved, what deficiencies are outstanding.

The idea of minimal competency as a requisite to high school graduation is also a matter of mastery of a certain body of behaviors. Tests used to determine whether the minimum has or has not been reached are criterion referenced. The behaviors to be exhibited and levels for minimums vary from location to location, but the principle of mastery remains for all minimal competency considerations.

It is not the purpose of the present discussion to defend or attack mastery learning as the goal of instruction for all learning. The authors leave the development of strategies for teaching and learning to curriculum developers. Our task is to develop strategies in collection and interpretation of data necessary to establish whether a student has or has not reached mastery. There seems to be no question that each classroom should be organized so that at least a part of the instruction is toward mastery; however, there are still many unanswered questions about teaching for mastery throughout the school program for all subjects.

FORMATIVE EVALUATION

An essential element of teaching for mastery or to a criterion of minimum acceptance is the organization of instruction around small units. Data collection for this kind of instructional organization needs to be done often, and interpretation made to direct further student

[3] Bloom, Hastings, and Madaus, *Formative and Summative Evaluation of Student Learning,* p. 43.

study and to coordinate teaching thrusts. The term *formative evaluation* has been given to techniques of assessing progress in this way and includes instruction with a loop back into further study on the same topic for students who have not attained mastery but instruction on new topics for those who have met mastery.

Formative evaluation takes place during the forming stage and provides for analysis during the learning process. The ongoing aspect of formative evaluation allows changes in instruction during the teaching process and thus supports needed adjustment in the program activities. Formative evaluation not only allows changes in curriculum for future students and classes but also for changes in instructional strategies for students in the present study. Formative evaluation facilitates curriculum construction, supports learning, and improves teaching.

Support of learning by formative evaluation comes through the use of test results to diagnose specific points of student difficulty. In the test results, the specific items missed or tasks which were inadequately treated can indicate what should be built into future learning strategies. Especially helpful is identification of lack of mastery for an element in a sequential learning pattern—a learning which is prerequisite to future learning. By providing **prescriptive learning** for diagnosed difficulties, the teacher supports present students' future study.

Teaching effectiveness can be improved through motivation of students. By using feedback that indicates difficulties, the teacher can give individual attention to a student who can see this interest as a teacher's sincere concern about him/her personally. Continuous feedback also allows the teacher to evaluate the changes made in the curriculum as a result of formative evaluation. Comparison to previous instructional strategies can be used to identify negative results as well as improvement in the program.

Instruction based on individual progress (individualized instruction) is based on feedback given by criterion-referenced measurement. Although not all mastery teaching is completely individualized, individually prescribed instruction becomes a part of all mastery teaching for those students who fail to meet the criterion for one or more tests. In both, the completely individualized instruction and the partially individualized approach, the formative nature of the evaluation and further instruction requires tests that give at frequent intervals a clear picture of what the student can do.

READING AND MATHEMATICS

Two subjects for which individual instruction seems to be most used are reading and mathematics. The sequential nature of learning in these subjects gives direction to arrangement of objectives into sequences, and it is easier to get general agreement that listed objectives are indeed the ones to be accomplished in study. Advocates of individualized instruction point out that the type of assessment needed (criterion referenced) is relevant for all students—those who are educationally advanced, those who have fallen behind in learning or have some handicap for learning, and those who are progressing at a normal rate. By keeping a direct relationship between what is to be learned (the objectives) and what students know (test scores), the teacher is better able to guide each student through a set of learning experiences in his/her own optimum time period.

This type of instruction breaks down large concepts into specific elements which are mastered one by one, thus leading to learning of the major concept. Within this structure, criterion-referenced tests play a crucial role by indicating specifically where a student has mastery and where more study is needed. If a decision is made to individualize instruction, then criterion-referenced tests are necessary to the process. On the other hand, if a decision to use criterion-referenced tests is made, the teacher is placed in a position of individualizing instruction for those topics or subjects which use criterion-referenced tests. The two go hand in hand.

Individual progress in these two important school subjects and the use of criterion-referenced tests as measuring devices can support the attempt to remove labels from students. Since the tests are not intended to give results to make a comparison of one student to another student or student groups but to standards set for mastery, comparison of a student to other students is reduced to comparison of each student to her/himself. Since future instruction is by prescription from past performance, the sequential skills are developed so that prerequisites are mastered before the student moves ahead.

Careful investigation of needed learning must be made so that all needed instruction is built into the learning activities, and testing materials are built to measure stated behavioral objectives. Two or more different sequences could conceivably be built for one large concept if different paths were developed. One person's view of the structure of the process of addition might be different from someone else's view. For example, one person might sequence a student through a set of learning experiences to teach addition using only positive whole numbers, while someone else might structure the learning to include all integers, including negative whole numbers, zero, and positive whole numbers. The difference in the instructional objectives would require entirely different criterion-referenced tests for the two situations.

Construction of criterion-referenced tests will be directed by the nature of the learning process expected from the instruction.

Classroom teachers who build their own tests should not have difficulty in coordinating the measurement and evaluation processes with the instruction process and the bridging element of objectives. Criterion-referenced tests prepared outside the classroom may or may not fit the specific instruction for a classroom. Outside criterion-referenced tests in reading and mathematics are more likely to fit a particular classroom than, say, a subject in social studies or a unit in elementary science; however, inspection of various instructional strategies for even the highly structured and sequential topics in mathematics reveals that many difficulties are associated with development of tests, especially criterion-referenced tests, to be used in many classrooms.

OTHER SUBJECTS

The difficulties associated with criterion-referenced assessment in reading and mathematics are magnified for other, less-structured subjects. However, each subject is built on a structure which could be used as a basis for extended study of topics within the broader subject area. Criterion-referenced assessment for that core of subject matter may be appropriate since all students would be expected to grasp the basics. For example, a concept which is used in a study of geography is the dependence of one person on other persons and dependence of others on that one person and the interdependence of countries as well as groups of persons in one country. To measure for mastery for all possible relationships of persons and countries is impossible. Development of the concept in general allows application in specific cases. It is not likely that the instruction should be pointed to each specific case, so testing for only the large concept for mastery may be appropriate procedure.

Testing for mastery should be used only when appropriate for the topic under study and for a clearly defined domain of behaviors. Certain tests in all subject areas are best interpreted by using a criterion as a reference. Basic concepts, certain bodies of knowledge, and particular skills can be considered as necessary components for further study, and the teacher needs to assess whether students have or have not achieved these components at acceptable levels. At the present time it seems that attempts to measure by criterion may be either inefficient or impossible beyond measurement of those basic knowledges, competencies, or skills expected from every student.

Devices to Measure

Tests which are to be interpreted by criterion referencing (objectives used as referents) are intended to measure what every student is expected to know. Therefore, these tests should consist of items written at the lowest acceptable performance level for the specific standards set in the behavioral objectives, since they are not intended to measure beyond the minimum acceptance level. The thrust of test construction is toward building a device that will generate information about whether a student can or cannot do those things expected from all students.

One of the first things a person must do when developing a criterion-referenced achievement test is to communicate in some way precisely what domain of behaviors is to be measured. As mentioned earlier, one way to do that would be through use of behavioral objectives, but conceivably a set of test specifications or some other plan could be used. In any case, statements in terms of observable behaviors will be required.

To interpret behaviors through objectives, some standard of acceptable performance must be set. The teacher's professional knowledge and experience must be brought into play because there is no other way to establish standards at this time. Standards may be set by stating the behavior which is to be exhibited "X" number of times with no errors, "X" number of times with an acceptable error number or error rate, number of words to be typed per minute, or any established measure that conveys to all concerned the lowest acceptable level of performance.

A situation must be arranged to allow the student to exhibit that s/he has developed competency at or above the established standard. Since our concern here is for tests (other data-collecting situations will be needed for some objectives), a testing device must be constructed which contains items at the minimum level with no items exceeding that level. The items must be homogeneous in that they are representative of the behavior to be exhibited. If the objective is:

> **A fifth grade student will be able to compute the area of five right triangles given the lengths of the two sides with no errors,**

then the triangles must all have one angle which is 90°. Likewise, items to test another objective must be relative to the behavior being measured, and there should be enough items to allow a clear decision as to whether the student has developed the required competency level or not.

The results of the testing session are compared to the predetermined acceptance level. In a truly criterion-referenced interpretation, the performance is judged as either passing criterion or not passing criterion. Some tests referred to as criterion referenced have levels of passing in addition to the single pass–no pass point. If a descriptor set is added to the satisfactory continuum, additional comparisons will need to be made. The interpretation is made by a comparison of the number of successes in the trials to the number of successes required for minimum acceptance or some other success rate set forth in the behavioral objective statement.

When building a test to be interpreted by criterion, it is important to realize that a test is not considered to be criterion referenced just because a cutoff point of 80 percent or 90 percent is associated with the final score interpretation. Only when a clear description of what the items are measuring is given can the test be truly criterion referenced. The purpose of the use of a criterion as a referent is to describe the status of each student who is being assessed as either meeting minimum level or not. To merely write items which are attached to a behavioral objective does not make the test a criterion-referenced test in the contemporary sense.

The descriptive explanation (specific table of specifications or a succinct behavioral objective) of what the test is to measure serves three purposes:

1. **It clarifies for the teacher what behaviors the test should measure.**
2. **It sets the boundaries for the material to be covered in the test.**
3. **It serves the score interpretation by associating different verbal statements with different scores.**

The definition of the behavior to be assessed by the test and the level of minimum acceptance sets the stage for test construction and score interpretation. The building of the test follows general test-building guidelines for writing directions for tests and item construction. The items to be included on the test must be homogeneous and at the level prescribed by the descriptive explanation. The interpretation of the score is taken up in the next section.

Interpreting Test Performance

The intended purpose of a criterion-referenced test is to measure what the teacher has determined ought to be taught and to assess whether or not students have learned at least the minimum. If the intended competencies are clearly defined and a test operationalizes the definition, then the scores of the test should be direct measures of the described behavior. Teachers use these measures in two ways. First, the teacher wants to check each student's performance score with the criterion set for acceptance of minimal competency. Second, the teacher will want to check the effectiveness of the instruction for students in general.

STUDENT EVALUATION

The first thing that a teacher does with a student's score on a criterion-referenced test is to compare the test score with the criterion point set for minimum acceptance. Those students who have met criterion performance have achieved an acceptable level for whatever behavior the test was designed to measure and are ready to proceed to a new learning task or sequence. Students who have not met criterion are given additional instruction on the same subject-matter topics.

A criterion-referenced test can be constructed to measure more than one objective. On a test of this kind, the items are arranged into subtests so that items do not overlap among objectives to be measured by the test. The test would appear to the student as one test, but the interpretation of scores would be by sets of items, each set of which is tied directly to an objective. The student could meet acceptable levels of performance on all subsets or pass some while not passing one or more other sets.

With this interpretation scheme, the classroom must be organized for instruction at more than one level. Either individual instruction or teaching in small, homogeneous groups must be arranged for the ongoing teaching-learning process. Formative evaluation is used to direct further study basing instruction on what the test scores reveal about student competencies.

Teaching in sequence means that each student who meets criterion will be assigned new reading, new activities (and/or lecture/didactic class instruction), and enough practice to prepare for the next test to measure achievement of criterion for the new topic. Instruction is made up of a series of these "teaching and then measuring" episodes. Reflection on the subject matter studied and student characteristics should tell the teacher whether or not this minimum type of learning is appropriate for the subject-matter and the students.

Students who have not met criterion are retaught the material. Hopefully, the new instruction will be different from the initial instruction and not be a recycling through the same experiences which were not successful the first time. After the student has completed the next instructional sequence, s/he is given a criterion-referenced test to determine whether or not the objective has been reached. Those who pass criterion go on to new learning while those who have not met criterion remain at the same instructional level.

The strategies for achieving mastery learning are many, and our topic of testing does not include an in-depth study of the instructional aspects of this type of teaching. The major problem in the development of a strategy is to find ways within the structure of the classroom to allow for altering the length of time individual student's need to achieve mastery and at the same time cover the material which is expected to be taught. Neither the problem of measurement nor the problem of instruction is easily solved, and much coordination is needed to take the results of testing (test scores), interpret what they mean, and then use them to direct future student learning.

PROGRAM EVALUATION

The assessment of student progress is an important component of educational evaluation. An equally important component of educational evaluation is assessing the effectiveness of the instructional program. Although judging the suitability of an educational program requires information from many sources, test data must be included since that information comes directly from the students. Since the schools exist for the students, the information which they give through their test scores must be considered to be of particular importance.

Although some program evaluations rest solely on measurement data, a better approach to assessment of most programs includes consideration of other contributing factors. Program evaluation is a highly technical process when implemented on a large scale. Such factors as student ability, student experiential background, program costs, morale of the teaching staff, possible alternate programs, teacher preparation, administrative support, and support of the community are only a few factors which evaluators include in a comprehensive evaluation procedure for judging program effectiveness.

Program evaluation at the classroom level (the evaluation which concerns our discussion) can be made by the teacher without considering each of these factors independently because decisions are made at the administrative level which provide a ready made structure within which the teacher must work. Since the behavioral objectives are set at the classroom level with regard to student characteristics, the effectiveness of the program can be judged best by the proportion of students who meet criterion on the tests and how far into the sequence students as a whole have moved. The teacher's close relationship with the components of this aspect of the evaluation process should allow a valid decision about the effectiveness of a particular program for a particular set of students.

To report to others about program effectiveness, the teacher has the problem of organizing a meaningful explanation of the results. If a clear description of what is to be attained (achieved) by the students has been made, reports giving percentages of those who met criterion seems to be most appropriate. Graphs (see Chapter 4) are also descriptive and easily understood by almost everyone and can be used to explain further.

A necessary part of the report will be a narrative by the teacher which gives further insight to program impact. The narrative will need to be different for different audiences, so the teacher will need to write in terms of those who will be reading and using the report. For example, curriculum persons will need information that differs from what parents will need, and interpretation must be keyed to the audience who will be using the judgment of evaluation to make educationally oriented decisions.

The diagnostic element of formative evaluation also reports program effectiveness and the impact of prescriptive teaching. All in all, the teacher should be receiving continuous evaluation of program effectiveness if the system is working as expected. Certainly, the key to valid evaluation at the classroom level is valid test data. The messages discerned by the teacher as s/he interprets the data form the basis for curriculum change for students in both the present and the future.

Considerations

When deciding about the kind of reference system to use to interpret classroom test scores, the teacher must consider the type of instruction and the nature of the subject matter. Certain advantages are associated with criterion-referenced interpretation, but certain disadvantages are also attached. The following two sections point up those aspects which all teachers must reflect on when deciding which reference system to use.

ADVANTAGES

Interpretation of scores from a true criterion-referenced test should indicate precisely what each student can do in terms of behaviors. Most of the advantages of this kind of interpretation are directly tied to that expectation, and the others are indirectly related to that measurement of behaviors. In general, the advantages of criterion-referenced measurement (CRM) are as follows:

1. **CRM can be used to measure attributes of the cognitive domain where mastery of certain material and skills is expected. This is particularly important because nearly all very early learning should be at mastery level and all subjects at all levels have certain material that must be mastered. For this reason, some criterion-referenced tests are needed for nearly all classroom testing programs.**
2. **CRM structures the measurement process so that assessment of affective attributes is facilitated. Testing in the affective domain is still one of the most difficult areas of assessment. It is difficult to measure these attributes because of the inner and personal nature of the traits. Another major difficulty is the problem of describing the attribute in**

a definition. The close relationship of the description and the measurement in CRM overcomes the second difficulty to a considerable degree.

3. CRM is useful for measuring in the psychomotor domain. Use of a criterion point as reference for measurement of physical competency and skill is a natural outcome for this type of performance. However, establishment of the point may be in terms of what others of similar characteristics have exhibited as typical performance, which brings in the aspect of norm-referenced measurement.

4. CRM indicates what specific tasks a student can perform. Since objectives have been stated in expected performance, and criterion points have been established, the measure (test score) allows direct interpretation of performance.

5. The tasks presented in CRM should be easily understood by the students. Since the test items must be at the minimum level for mastery, the items should be such that all students have the experience and practice to understand what the teacher is asking for in the response.

6. CRM serves to measure the material that every student is expected to master. This is important to provide information about present functioning of those aspects basic to the course of study.

7. CRM provides the kind of data most needed for formative evaluation. Formative evaluation is implemented to direct changes needed in the intructional program. CRM provides a large portion of the input for the ongoing evaluation during the forming process of instruction.

8. CRM works hand in hand with individualized instruction. When instruction is organized for individuals, the teacher needs to know what a student can and can not do to prescribe new instructional strategies. The interpretation of CRM provides the needed information for this phase of individualized instruction.

9. A score at or above criterion indicates a level of performance prerequisite to some other higher level of performance. Sequentially organized subjects can use CRM to determine when specified learning has been mastered, and when it is time to commence new learning activities.

10. A given student does not compete with peers or a set of peers but rather in reaching a goal that in the teacher's opinion the student can reach. Some pressure may be relieved within some students if they do not find themselves competing with classmates for test scores and find that competition is transfered to rate of progress for each student against himself or herself.

11. The results of a criterion-referenced test that measures in the cognitive domain can be diagnostic. CRM for content subjects and cognitive skill development can be interpreted to identify specific objectives where more time is needed to achieve mastery and specific points which need to be given attention.

LIMITATIONS

Interpretation of test scores from a true criterion-referenced test fails to reveal a student's level of achievement. Although the scores indicate whether a student has achieved a certain objective or not, the scores do not allow for assessment of overall achievement. Most of the limitations of CRM are either directly or indirectly tied to this deficiency. In general, the limitations of CRM are as follows:

1. Scores from CRM do not indicate how good or poor a student's level of achievement is. To know that a student is proficient in a specific learning area does not indicate how good or poor the student's level of functioning is. This component is needed to make scores meaningful. The statement that a student knows addition facts must be interpreted at some time in regard to the student's age, grade level, and experiential background. Even to report a student's weight as 76 pounds means little until information such as height, age, and body build are given. Much the same holds true for CRM test scores: at some point in time the idea of relative performance must enter into the interpretation. It may be included when setting the minimum acceptance level as criterion or after the scores are reported.

2. Relatively few areas of cognitive learning and only parts of other areas are amenable to being reduced solely to a list of specific behavioral objectives. Lists of objectives at any level are rarely, if ever, exhaustive. A very large part of many subject topics resist any efforts to be reduced to a set of behavioral objectives. Since general objectives cannot be written in behavioral terms, CRM cannot be used to measure large portions of subject matter in which objectives cannot be stated in specific behaviors.

3. Instruction solely to a set of specific behaviors does not allow for expansion of learning by taking advantage of ongoing classroom activities. Many outcomes of instruction are a result of ongoing instruction that allows the teacher to adjust teaching to take advantage of flexibility allowed by general objective statements. In this sense, teaching solely to a set of behavioral objectives may restrict the teacher, the teaching and, in turn, the learning.

4. If all teaching is tied to specific behavioral objectives, then teaching may be suppressed and overall learning reduced. If the teacher is limited to teaching mastery of behavioral objectives, s/he cannot use opportune moments to develop students' overall understanding and identify relationships and structures.

5. A question arises about whether the standards are realistic. Although much attention is given to setting standards, there is always a question about the criterion set for interpretation. Since the criterion is the key to criterion-referenced measurement, the interpretation of scores by criterion is only as good as the process used to set the criterion. Hopefully, the process has enough substance to generate valid interpretation of scores from CRM.

6. Use of CRM exclusively does not allow a teacher to compare students with other students outside of the classroom where instruction took place. Comparison to an absolute standard for a criterion gives no indication of how student performance relates to performance of students throughout the nation or some more limited geographic region.

CONCLUSION

True criterion-referenced measures allow for interpretation that can be highly useful for some classroom measurement and evaluation. When the tests generate valid data about cognitive achievement or skill development, they can tell specifically what a student can or can not do. This information is especially valuable when certain learning is:

1. **prerequisite to other learning, or**
2. **requisite to special functioning.**

For some learning, the need is for mastery. For example, a student must know how to subtract before using the subtractive algorithm for division. Mastery of a prerequisite is necessary in this case and is also requisite to some functioning. For example, when a teacher's major objective is to prepare each student to act as a first-aid person on an emergency vehicle, to be considered qualified each student must master certain skills and have particular knowledge by the end of instruction. When agreement is reached about what those needed skills are and what knowledge is needed, instruction is pointed toward mastery for each student. CRM seems appropriate, since the instructor needs information about what a student can do and to be sure that the student has achieved mastery before being classed as qualified. To know 70 percent of what is needed is not enough for on-the-job performance as an aid person. Complete mastery of the material is requisite for job performance on an emergency vehicle.

Criterion-referenced tests do not produce scores that give the desired information for all questions asked about student performance. When the need is to know levels of knowledge or achievement in a broadly defined scope, criterion referencing cannot produce meaningful scores. In fact, the value of CRM lies in the measurement of specifics. When there is no need for each student to learn the same things that all other students learn, interpretation to a criterion is not only undesirable but impossible. In achievement for most subjects, learning is expected to take diverse directions; therefore, instruction and, in turn, interpretation of test scores should allow for differences. CRM can not do that.

Criterion-referenced strategies seem to be especially useful for measurement in the **affective** domain. Although classroom teachers are not expected to build devices to measure interests, attitudes, and values, student dispositions are important to classroom functioning. Information from such devices is often available for teachers to use in planning instruction for students.

Use of CRM for skill development serves the teacher who is dealing with objectives in the **psychomotor** domain. Teachers will be using devices made outside the classroom for measurement of both cognitive skills, such as oral reading, and motor skills, such as physical development, typing, and welding, as well as tests which they prepare especially for their students. In most cases standards are easily set for measurement in this area and criterion-referenced interpretation of scores is a useful tool.

8 Norm-Referenced Interpretation

The descriptive expression "norm referenced" is presently used to identify a system of interpreting test scores. The central idea behind norm referencing is the use of the performance of some group of subjects to establish norms that are then used to interpret an individual student's test performance. In contrast to criterion-referenced interpretation, which uses absolute standards, the norms are not intended to be standards in and of themselves. Student performance in absolute terms is left for the teacher to evaluate by using data about characteristics of the set of students who took the test and comparing their test performance to performance and characteristics of the norm group. If the class is its own norm group, then the interpretation is done somewhat differently. The distribution of the class test scores is used to interpret each individual score within the context of group performance if the class serves as the norm group. The comparison of one score in a distribution to the general performance of all in that group is made only in regard to relative standing. Measurements of classroom performance which use the class as a norm group will differ according to the makeup of the group, thus requiring the judgment of the performance to be made according to standards external to the set of students who took the test. This judgment is usually made to the standard set by the teacher, and performance is not judged solely in regard to relative performance.

The principle of interpreting student performance to a norm or set of norms dates back to the second decade of this century. Psychologists needed a way to interpret scores on newly constructed psychological tests, and use of an average as a normal score seemed to be the best way to make relative statements about different levels of performance. A person's performance interpretation was best thought of as relative to the way others performed or behaved.

From the late thirties or early forties, a large portion of interpretation of test performance has been made with some form of norm referencing. A major criticism of norm referencing, even during this time period, stemmed from an idea that if a group set its own norms, then some students were guaranteed high levels of performance while, at the same time, some were doomed to failure. The way that some persons used a norm-referencing system supported this concept; however, it was the use of the system, not the system itself that was at fault. There is no built-in element of norm referencing that interprets the students' scores as being high or low in absolute terms. Another criticism was that norms become standards and that any group being tested sets its own standards without any external input to set appropriate standards. If norms were used as standards, the error again was in the use of the norms, not the norm referencing itself. The system had no way of controlling how it was used, and certain misunderstandings led to misuse of norms in interpreting test scores. The nearly complete use of norm referencing continued through the 1960s, but the idea of criterion referencing began to get much support in the early 1970s.

Criterion referencing was championed by educators who were convinced that any student at a given grade level could learn any body of content for that grade level, although some would move through the sequence rapidly while others would require more time in varying amounts. With mastery learning, the teacher needed tests that generated information about how much a student knew about a clearly defined body of content and behaviors. Since norm referencing could not do that, another kind of reference system was needed for some tests. With the criterion-reference interpretation, expectations could be set in terms of absolutes, and each student could be checked carefully and often about how s/he was progressing to mastery. Norm referencing could not do that.

Today, norm referencing is considered to be the traditional system for interpreting test scores. Criterion referencing is considered by some as innovative, but as pointed out earlier, it was the first method used to interpret student performance. Even during the period from the 1910s to the 1970s certain performance was judged to absolute standards which served as criteria. For example, a typing student was expected to type a specified number of words per minute with rate reduction for errors. Students' products—speeches, essays, art work, cakes, musical renditions, and such—were judged against criteria rather than averages. Expected performance, although stated in absolute terms, was determined largely from how students had performed previously.

Norm referencing has been used almost exclusively by standardized test makers, and since it was used by test specialists, other educators assumed that norm referencing should be used to the near exclusion of judging to absolute standards. Today, the classroom teacher is well-advised to select from the two referencing systems and for each test to apply the system that is appropriate for the use to be made of the test scores. This chapter gives attention to that part of the testing program that generates scores indicating differences. This kind of testing requires reference to norms for score interpretation. The teacher is expecting students to show satisfactory performance, but in different degrees. Effective teaching in this type of instruction based on a range of student ability and motivation will cause scores to be spread widely across the score continuum.

Norms as Referents

In the strictest sense, all tests are written with an eye to what groups of students with particular sets of characteristics are expected to do, but with norm-referenced test interpretation, a direct relationship is established between each score on the test and the relationship of that score to an average or set of norms. Educational objectives are the basis for the test items, but the general objectives may be stated without a preset level of acceptable performance and, consequently, be more general than behavioral objectives. Subjects that are not totally made up of a body of content that must be learned in its entirety by all students (mastered) allow for students' behavior at many levels to be considered as satisfactory.

When the teacher knows in general what classroom instruction is to produce, s/he will need to direct teaching to helping each student reach her/his full potential. Determination of how well students have achieved will need to be interpreted to something other than an absolute standard. By using norms or norm referents, the teacher can write test items and relate them to objectives more generally so that an overall picture of how a student achieved is produced rather than a list of behaviors that have been successfully attained. Comparison of the test results to peer performance becomes the system of score interpretation. The principle used in building norm-referenced tests is the same principle used when measuring physical properties. The resulting measure (the score) is intended to be an indication of how much someone or something has of the attribute that the measuring device is measuring. A thermometer measures the amount of heat, and a history test measures the amount of history achievement. For this type of testing, a test-score distribution should have a wide range if the students being tested form a heterogeneous group. Even with a relatively homogeneous group of students, the scores that measure relative amounts of knowledge and skill should have differences and a rather wide score range.

Relative Testing

Those who advocate the use of norm referencing for classroom tests point up that criterion-referenced tests generate test results (scores) that are good for telling whether or not a student has reached proficiency on a set of behaviors but that they lack information about the level of achievement. Within the structure of many classrooms, each student is provided an opportunity to achieve at a maximum for the given potential. The assumption is that there should not be any built-in part of the school program that restricts what students learn or the skills they develop and that each student should be encouraged to go as far beyond minimum achievement as possible.

TEACHING FOR MAXIMUM

For many years, educators have been developing school programs intended to allow each student the opportunity to develop to full potential. There is not common agreement about how this should be accomplished, but the differences lie in how this is to be done, not in the final aim. The two different approaches to maximum achievement can be explained in terms of what opportunities the program provides. One approach encourages vertical development while the other encourages horizontal development. In either case, the doors are opened with opportunities for students to move as far beyond mastery of minimums as possible.

Vertical Development

A program designed to move students vertically is organized so that students are not limited in what topics to study. If there is a sequence to long-term learning, it is not interrupted at any point in the instructional program because of a grade level or age division. One topic is not considered to be a first-grade topic, another topic to be studied in the second grade, and so on.

The program sequence can be different for every student, but common experiences are shared by certain groups of students. The class does not move through topics at the same rate, although instruction is not structured as formally as individually prescribed instruction. For example, a primary-level reading class may use instructional readers at several levels. The class may be organized into groups and/or individualized according to reading ability.

In the case of vertical development, students are placed at various levels in a teaching sequence with the hope that each student will reach minimum levels by the time the course is completed. By the end of instruction many students should be far beyond the minimum expected for all students. Teachers who use this approach without regard to later instruction may place a hardship on subsequent teachers who do not organize their teaching in the same way. Articulation of instructional methods between classes should be made so that the student is not placed in a bad position by different approaches in the grade sequence. Assuming that vertical development is encouraged within a school building, interpretation of scores at the end of one grade level is crucial to indicate to the new teacher where instruction should commence in the sequence.

Horizontal Development

A program designed to move students horizontally is organized such that students are not given new topics to study. Instead the scope of topics that are presented is broadened for in-depth learning through extension of experiences within topics. The use of enrichment materials and activities is intended to give deeper comprehension within each topic studied. The premise for this type of instruction is based on the principle that mastery learning of basic knowledge and skills, although necessary, needs to be supplemented in different ways for different students. The thrust is toward an in-depth understanding of topics rather than a series of learning experiences which culminate with mastery (minimum) levels.

Students are, in general, kept on the same topics in the classroom study; however, the horizontally organized instructional program is different for each student. Elementary school classrooms use "the math corner," "the science corner," or classroom library to foster horizontal learning. Special collections of materials relating to topics of study but at different levels allow motivated students to attain a deeper understanding of topics. At the secondary level teachers may have more opportunity to do this with individuals as student interests develop and students begin to form some ideas about present interests about future careers.

In horizontal development there is much learning beyond the level of the mastery of material that each student is expected to assimilate. The most advanced student in the class should be far beyond the least advanced, but there is no reason to believe that the one has failed because of his relative position in the class. Hopefully, everyone can exhibit satisfactory performance but at different degrees.

Testing for Relative Standing

When teaching has been organized around instruction for maximum learning, the measuring instrument used to quantify a student's knowledge or skill is designed differently from the criterion-referenced testing device. The scores from the test must give more information about the student than a test designed to measure for mastery of a minimum amount of competency. The test scores should provide the teacher and each student an indication of each student's achievement relative to group performance. The test needs to be built of tasks that collectively generate scores reflecting different levels of achievement. Measurement is accomplished by establishing a reference point based on average performance of a particular group of students. From this point a scale is devised based on the way scores fall in relation to that point, and students' scores are reported accordingly.

For standardized tests, norm-group data are used to establish norm tables to place each individual score in relation to the position of that score in the norm-group distribution. The norm table used to interpret the scores ranges from a very low point, which is only rarely reached by any test taker, to a very high point, which also is rarely reached by any test taker. The rest of the scores fall somewhere between these two extremes. In this way the student should be measured at the maximum level of achievement. When interpreting a single obtained score from a student in a classroom, the teacher compares what that student did with the performance of the norm group by placing that score in the norm tables. That tells the teacher what that student would have scored if s/he were a member of the norm group.

For classroom tests, the score distribution of obtained student scores allows the teacher to use the basic principle explained above by considering the set of scores the same way as a set from a norm group. Hopefully, the teacher has been successful in constructing a test that incorporates the principles needed to establish an appropriate ceiling and an appropriate floor for test scores, taking into consideration the characteristics of the students and subject matter studied. If so, the score should place each student in relation to all other students who took the test so that the class is ordered by test scores in the same order that they have achieved. Also, each student should have an indicator which points out her/his relative placement.

Testing for determination of maximum student achievement is intended to expand the testing program the same way that teaching for maximum achievement expands the classroom instruction. If teaching beyond mastery of essentials is the goal, then criterion-referenced tests will not be appropriate measuring devices for classroom tests. The same type of item (multiple-choice, true/false, etc.) could be used in both kinds of tests. In fact, the exact same item could appear in both kinds of tests. The basic difference involves what the item is to measure. Criterion-referenced test items are written so that satisfactory performance shows minimum level of development. Norm-referenced test items are written so that many levels of achievement can be ascertained.

Research indicates that the best approach to item difficulty for norm-referenced tests is to use items that are of about medium difficulty. Items with that level of difficulty will best reflect the actual attainment levels as it varies within the group. An item that is too easy and, thus, is answered correctly by nearly all students does not test to students' expected level of attainment. An item that is too difficult and, thus, answered incorrectly by nearly all of the students does not really assess what students should be reasonably expected to know. Neither of these kinds of items will be able to contribute to distinguishing differences among the students' levels of achievement.

Devices to Measure

Tests that are to be interpreted by norm referencing (average referents) are intended to measure how a student's performance compares with his/her peer group—either classmates or a set of peers—which is used as a norm group. Therefore, these tests should consist of items that collectively allow a student to reveal achievement at any level. They are intended to measure achievement from the lowest to the highest possible levels. In practice the floor and ceiling for the test are set so that each student will be measured at his/her level of achievement. For example, a standardized third-grade spelling test would exclude two sets of words: first, those words that nearly all third-grade students know how to spell and, second, those words considered too difficult for most third-grade students. The thrust for this kind of test would be to answer the question, What level of spelling achievement does this student have compared to third-grade students in general? Word lists that have been assigned for study in class are expected to be mastered, and the final weekly spelling test is likely to be a criterion-referenced test. Six-week or semester spelling tests could be either norm referenced or criterion referenced at the choice of the teacher.

One of the first things a person must do when developing a norm-referenced achievement test is to communicate in some way the content and behaviors to be covered on the test. Tables of specifications are developed to direct writing of items that will weight content according to relative importance and select test behaviors from appropriate behavior classes. If items of appropriate difficulty (no items which nearly all students would answer correctly and no items which nearly all students would answer incorrectly) are selected, the test should generate scores that reveal differences in levels of achievement and can be used to order students according to the differences.

To interpret behavior by norms, the teacher must select some reference group. For classroom tests the class serves as its own reference group, and for standardized tests the norms in the test manual are used. In contrast to criterion referencing, norm-referenced classroom tests do not have predetermined performance standards. After the test has been administered, the scores are organized and transformed into meaningful statistics, depending primarily on who will be using the scores. Reports will interpret each score in terms of how it compares to the rest of the scores.

The principles used for construction of norm-referenced tests are many and too detailed for discussion here. A review or study of test construction is recommended if these principles do not readily come to mind at this time. Coverage of test construction can be found in another issue of this series[1] or in some other resource book on building classroom tests. Because criterion-referenced and norm-referenced tests measure achievement similarly, their formats and test items tend to be similar, and the instruments for both kinds of tests look very much alike. However, there are two major differences: (1) how items are selected and (2) the interpretation of obtained scores.

The test builder for both types of tests selects items from a domain of tasks that describe performance. The criterion-referenced test samples from a clearly defined domain of actions which exemplify minimum level of conduct. For the norm-referenced test the sample is taken from the complete domain of subject-matter knowledge and behaviors that describe the classroom instructional course of study.

Interpreting Test Performance

Since a test is a measuring device, its function is to quantify the amount of a specific trait that each student has. Measurement answers questions like, How much height does Dan have? How much spelling (or history, physics, etc.) achievement does Dan have? How many free throws can Dan make in thirty seconds? Obviously, tests cannot serve as a measuring device for all student characteristics that are of concern to teachers, but they serve to quantify many attributes important to student progress through the process of education—especially measurement of achievement.

[1] Charles D. Hopkins and Richard L. Antes, *Classroom Testing: Construction* (Itasca, Ill.: F. E. Peacock Publishers, Inc., 1979).

Test scores reflect little meaning in and of themselves. As with other measures, they must be explained in meaningful terms. Even a well-understood measure of weight means little before a frame of reference is established. For example, Dan's weight of 121 pounds must be translated into meaningful terms by getting answers to such questions as How old is Dan? How tall is Dan? What is his body build? A weight of 121 pounds for a slightly built fifteen-year-old student who is five feet six inches tall is a much different measure than the same reading of 121 pounds for a ten-year-old student who is four feet four inches tall. A Dan who is a professional basketball player should be able to make many more free throws in a limited time period than a Dan who is a middle-fielder on a junior high school soccer team. Measures of weight and free-throwing ability must be interpreted within the framework of some reference system (probably norm-referenced) that makes them understandable. Likewise, measures of achievement must be interpreted in terms of some reference system if the teaching has been for maximum performance.

Measures from many classroom tests should use norm-referenced interpretation as a frame of reference to make students' scores meaningful. A set of scores may be used to compare a student's performance with his/her peer group. The mathematical techniques and graphical representations presented in Chapters 4, 5, and 6 are used to make scores meaningful for evaluative procedures and purposes. Interpretation should be conducted, keeping in mind which educational questions are to be answered, what information is needed, and who the teacher will be reporting to. The use of the scores is incorporated into the evaluation procedures for assessing student progress and evaluation of program effectiveness, which are discussed separately in the next two sections.

STUDENT EVALUATION

The simplest way to view a student score in terms of other student scores is to arrange all scores in order from highest to lowest. Known as ordering, this procedure gives meaning to a score by investigating where that score appears in the order. The number of scores above and below each score can be counted, and the relative position of each score can be determined.

A more formal approach extends the ordering by assigning a rank number (see Figure 8.1) to each score. The highest score receives a rank of one, the second score a rank of two, and so forth through the total number of scores. To make the report of a rank meaningful, the number of scores being ranked must be given. If a score is sixth in a set of fourteen

Raw Score X	Rank	
60	1	
58	2	
57	3	
55	4	
53	5.5	
53	5.5	
52	7.5	
52	7.5	
49	9	
48	10	
46	11.5	
46	11.5	
45	13.5	
45	13.5	This is
43	15.5	←your
43	15.5	score
42	18	
42	18	
42	18	
40	21	
40	21	
40	21	
39	23.5	
39	23.5	
38	25	
35	26	
32	27	
30	28	
28	29.5	
28	29.5	

Figure 8.1 A list of the general science test scores and the associated ranks used to report relative performance to a student.

scores, the report would be a rank of six out of fourteen students, or "Veronica's rank is six out of the fourteen students in her class."

The evaluation of an individual student is of importance not only to the teacher but to the student and his/her set of parents. Ranks are generally well understood by all except very young children and a few parents, but some explanation of a rank may be needed so that the student and parent understand what a rank means. A report that includes a rank along with the number ranked gives information needed to place a score in relation to all other scores based on order and provides a very good indication of individual performance compared to general group performance. Ordering scores and assigning ranks are most important to those persons who are concerned with students individually rather than collectively. Although other interpretive means are used, listing students' ranks gives easily understood information that can be used to compare one performance to the group's performance.

Frequency Distribution

A listing of the number of times (frequency) each score appears in a set of scores organized in sequence (see "Frequency Distribution" in Chapter 4) gives an overview of all scores and allows each student to isolate an obtained score in the distribution and compare it to all the other scores since all scores appear. The list could be in tabular form as shown in Figure 8.2, and each student could locate his/her own position in the frequency distribution. The score 43 has been marked for a student who obtained that score.

Score	f	
60	1	
58	1	
57	1	
55	1	
53	2	
52	2	
49	1	
48	1	
46	2	
45	2	This is
43	2	←your
42	3	score
40	3	
39	2	
38	1	
35	1	
32	1	
30	1	
28	2	

Figure 8.2 Report of a student's score on the general science test.

A frequency distribution can also be presented in graphic form (see Histogram and Frequency Polygon in Chapter 4) for score interpretation. A graph can be prepared for duplication and each student's score can be added to one copy of the graph as a record for each student. The score 43 has been added to the graph in Figure 8.3 to indicate how this could be done for a report to the student who scores that value. If each student is provided a graph with his/her test score marked, a direct report is made about relative standing on a test. This form of report

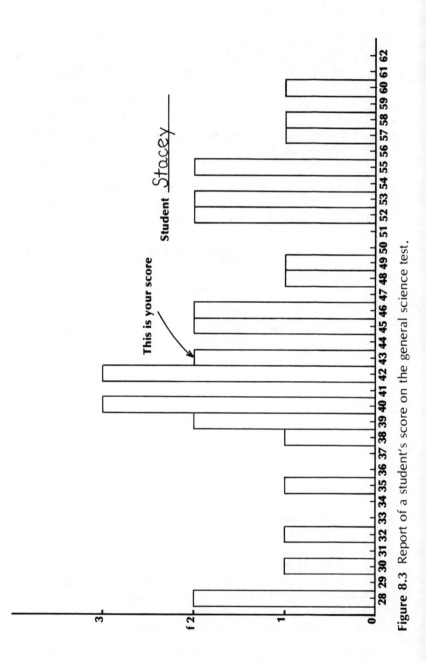

Figure 8.3 Report of a student's score on the general science test.

would be used for major tests and reports over grading periods but not for quizzes and daily work unless the teacher sees a special need for it.

Presenting the frequency distribution in tabular or graphic form gives the reader a picture for a quick analysis of test data. Students and parents are generally more concerned about how a score is related to the total performance of the tested group than to other particular scores. Thus, the frequency distribution is especially valuable to reveal the meaning of one student's score compared to the group performance. Classroom results from standardized tests can be reported by placing each student's score on a frequency distribution of norm values. Results from classroom tests can be reported the same way, thus allowing quick interpretation of one score by a student and parents.

Standard Scores

Standard scores (see Chapter 5) are derived scores based on the positions of scores measured in standard deviation units from the mean value. They are widely used in standardized testing but also can be used by the teacher to report classroom performance. A reported standard score locates a student's score in a distribution in standard deviation units from the mean value.

Since each distribution of test scores has its own mean and standard deviation, the student cannot derive meaning directly from raw test scores. However, if all raw scores for all tests are reported in the same standard score frame of reference, the student has specific direction for interpreting test performance. The teacher as well as the student is also able to average test scores meaningfully if scores are reported in a standard score framework. Raw scores from distributions having different means and different standard deviations cannot be averaged meaningfully.

The Z-score $[Z = 10(z) + 50]$ is recommended as the appropriate standard score to use for reporting performance on classroom tests. Z-scores serve the same purpose as z-scores and are based on the same principle; however, they have the advantages of being always positive, being expressed in larger values and not having decimal values.

Percentile Rank

The percentile rank (see Chapter 6) indicates the percentage of all the scores in a frequency distribution that falls below a given raw score. Teachers rarely use percentile ranks for reporting scores from a classroom test. When external norms are used for schoolwide tests or standardized tests, the percentile rank is often used to interpret a student's test score. The percentile rank gives the percentage of students in the norm group who scored at or below a specific score.

If a set of scores from a classroom is transformed to a set of percentile ranks by use of outside norms, there is no relationship within the class percentile ranks since the interpretation is external to the class performance. If every student scored the same value on the test, each student would receive the same percentile rank from the standardized test norm table. The set of percentile ranks could be restricted to a small range of values or could range widely through the 100-unit scale of percentile ranks.

Percentile ranks for a classroom test can be used if the teacher considers this to be a good way of reporting performance. A clear perception of how this differs from a percentage of correct responses must be understood by the reader of the report. If there is a question about whether it will be understood, an explanation should accompany reports of percentile ranks. This also holds true when results of standardized tests are reported in percentile ranks.

Stanines

A test score can be interpreted in general terms by reporting a stanine (see Chapter 6). A stanine, which is short for standard nine, can have a value from 1 to 9. Since stanines are associated with a band of values rather than a point on a scale, the report is in general terms. Teachers can report scores for classroom tests in stanines to avoid pointing up small differences among scores and thus reduce the use of comparison of one student's performance to another student's performance as students sometimes do.

Parents and students can interpret broad categories of low, average, and high for test performance. Further divisions could be:

Stanines 1, 2, 3,	as	lowest, lower, low
Stanines 4, 5, 6,	as	low average, average, high average
Stanines 7, 8, 9	as	high, higher, highest

If results of classroom tests are reported in stanines and students and parents learn how to use them, reports of results for standardized tests will also be more meaningful to them. Norms for many standardized tests are available in stanines and are being widely used because of the ability to communicate general test performance meaningfully.

PROGRAM EVALUATION

Norm referencing for classroom tests does not provide a direct connection between objectives and test performance. This is the primary reason why the need for criterion referencing resulted in a movement to interpretation to a specific domain of behaviors. The deficiency of a norm-referenced test which causes the greatest doubt about its ability to give information about program effectiveness is the question about what the test measures. Does the test provide a clear description of what the test taker's performance really indicates?

If someone wants to establish a direct relationship between test items and objectives, then s/he will not see any way to use norm-referenced test scores to indicate program effectiveness. If someone is willing to agree that professional educators are knowledgeable in subject-matter and test theory, then norm-referenced classroom tests can be used to provide information about program effectiveness.

The device that establishes a connecting link between objectives and norm-referenced test scores is the table of specifications. The table directs the writing of test items to measure appropriate subject-matter topics and behaviors. If the items are written to these points, then the test scores will give information about how effective the school program has been in moving students toward objectives set for them.

The process of education is designed to serve the educational needs of students. From these needs, teachers set student aims expressed as instructional objectives. From the objectives a school program is organized through a set of activities intended to move students to attainment of the objectives. Tests collect information about the level of attainment. From this information and other information gathered from students, teachers and administrators evaluate how well the objectives were reached. If the tests are based on objectives, the scores reflect the contribution of the program experiences to acquisition of needed knowledge and skills.

The use of norm-referenced test scores along with other data from nontesting procedures provides a much broader base for evaluative techniques than does a restricted dependence on criterion-referenced tests alone. Evaluation may best be thought of as the determination of the worth of something. In terms of testing this seems to point to the development and implementation of evaluative procedures that use all available information.

Properly selected standardized tests can indicate the success of a program. Overall performance can be interpreted by comparing the overall results of testing for a classroom or several classrooms to standardized test norms. Care must be taken to establish the validity of the test for the students. Age level, experiential background, scholastic aptitude, cultural background, and level of mental functioning must all be considered to achieve optimal validity.

Standardized test scores could be distributed as stanines, Z-scores, or percentile ranks and compared to known values for distributions of these scores. For example, the class test scores could be categorized by stanines using the norm group values that appear in the test manual. The scores should be about 4 percent for stanines 1 and 9, 6-7 percent for stanines 2 and 8, 12 percent for stanines 3 and 7, 17-18 percent for stanines 4 and 6, and 20 percent for stanine 5. Z-scores should be distributed about as normal curve values. Likewise, percentile ranks for the class should conform to the 100-point scale.

Standardized test scores and norms should not be used to set standards for an individual student or classes of students. Most standardized test norms are reported from norm groups intended to be representative of the nation as a whole. Geographic selection factors usually give classes of students a set of characteristics much different from those of a national sample. For example, fourth-grade students from a small rural town in mid-America are likely to have much different characteristics from fourth-grade students in a large industrial city in the South. Even rural students in Indiana are quite different on many characteristics from rural students in Utah.

Standardized tests which have norm-group tables for regions, subcultures, or other characteristics may be closer to being valid for classroom use, but the teacher must still make a judgment about how his/her students compare to norm-group characteristics. Averages for a standardized test may be unrealistically high for some groups and too low for other classrooms. For these reasons, the effectiveness of a teacher should never be judged in terms of how the scores of students compare to norm values for a standardized test. Although some norms for standardized tests have been used to set standards for students, they were not created for that purpose, and they were used incorrectly when employed as standards. They do serve a valuable service to the teacher who needs to compare the performance of one student or a classroom of students to that of an external norm group.

Considerations

When making a decision about the kind of reference system to use to interpret scores from classroom tests, the teacher must consider the type of instruction and the nature of the subject matter. Certain advantages are associated with norm-referenced interpretation, but this interpretation also has certain disadvantages. The following two sections point up those aspects that all teachers must reflect on when deciding which reference system to use.

ADVANTAGES

Interpretation of test scores from a norm-referenced test should assess a student attribute as it relates to other students. Most of the advantages of norm-referenced interpretation are directly tied to the test's ability to reveal levels of achievement, and the others are indirectly related to a report of relative student status. In general, the advantages of norm-referenced measurement (NRM) are as follow:

1. **NRM can be used to measure attributes of the cognitive domain where each student is allowed and encouraged to learn at his/her maximum potential. This is particularly important after students have learned the basics or core knowledge associated with each school topic and subject area. For this reason some norm-referenced tests are needed for nearly all classrooms because teachers rarely, if ever, put a ceiling on what a student is to learn.**
2. **NRM is especially valuable for the higher levels of the cognitive domain as student development focuses on complex learning strategies. As teaching moves from mastery of the basics or material to be learned by each student, referencing to a criterion is no longer effective interpretation.**
3. **NRM can be used when general objectives are used to direct the classroom instruction. If a set of behavioral objectives is considered to be a limiting factor to effective teaching, the teacher can use general objectives to structure instruction and allow him/her the freedom to make judgments within the instructional programs.**
4. **The distribution of test scores for norm referencing can be used as a device to assess an individual student's test performance. Group performance can be used to establish the status of each member of the group. If external norms are used, the student's performance can be established within that outside group.**
5. **NRM is especially valuable when a set of students is moved through an instructional sequence together, but students are expected to perform at different levels or to different degrees. For this type of instructional scheme a test needs to be able to measure a wide range of performance.**
6. **By use of a table of specifications, tests which are to be interpreted by norms can be built to adequately measure any given body of content and any set of behaviors. Norm-referenced measurement allows for a frame of reference not restricted to a direct connection between test items and a specific behavioral objective.**
7. **NRM is effective for testing for selection of candidates for particular assignments or tracks within a school system. Norm-referenced tests are excellent tools for selecting a predetermined number of subjects to undertake some particular study or sequence of studies.**

LIMITATIONS

Interpretation of test scores by norm-referencing fails to give a direct measure of achievement in absolute terms. Although the good test is built from a table of specifications to relate content taught to content measured, the test score can not be connected to a set of observable objectives. Most of the limitations of NRM are either directly or indirectly tied to this deficiency. In general, the limitations of NRM are as follows:

1. NRM is not appropriate for measuring mastery of certain material and skills. The test score gives no indication of what a student can do in absolute terms and does not allow for judgment about performance in specifics.
2. If material or topics are sequenced, NRM can not be used satisfactorily to indicate when a student is ready to move from one topic to another. If the ability to attain a second skill rests on being able to perform a first skill, then information other than that generated by interpreting to norms is needed.
3. NRM has only limited value for measuring in the affective and psychomotor domains. The need for a clear description of the measured attribute in the affective domain requires information that NRM cannot deliver. Measurement in the psychomotor domain requires a clearly defined criterion point for interpretation. Norms can be used to establish a criterion but can not be used in the final measurement interpretation.
4. NRM can not indicate specific tasks a student can perform and does not allow interpretation of performance directly from test scores.
5. Since NRM test items go beyond measurement of minimum acceptable performance, the tasks in the items are more difficult to set. Ambiguity about the task in a test item may be greater in NRM than in CRM.
6. Competition for high test scores among some students may result because of the relative measurement procedures.

CONCLUSION

Norm-referenced tests allow for interpretation that can be highly useful for some classroom measurement and evaluation. When the tests generate valid data about cognitive achievement or skill development, they can tell what one student can do in relation to what other students can do. This information is especially valuable when:

1. teaching and, in turn, learning has been directed to the maximum level, or
2. students are to be selected according to how they perform relative to peer performance.

For some learning, the need is for maximum amounts. For example, when basic needs for knowledge and skill have been met, students are encouraged to go as far as they can to extend their performance levels. The social studies teacher wants students to understand many aspects of interrelationships of the societal, economic, and political factors that led to the Civil War and does not place a limit on any student's learning level. NRM seems to be appropriate since the study has been such that wide variance in performance is expected. Since NRM utilizes tests with no ceiling and measures over a wide range, logic tells us that it should be used when teaching has been directed the same way.

Norm-referenced tests do not produce scores that tell specifically what a student can or can not do. Since some questions asked about student performance pertain to what a student can do, NRM does not generate scores that give the desired information for all questions about student performance. In fact, the value of NRM lies in the measurement of relative standing. When there is the need for students to learn to mastery or learn a body of content in its entirety, interpretation by norms is impossible. Much learning for very young children is directed to mastery, and introductory learning in any new undertaking is pointed toward assimilation of a specific body of basic knowledge and understanding and interpretation should be about what specific things a student knows and can do. NRM cannot do that.

Combining the conclusion section for criterion-referenced interpretation with the above conclusion section for norm-referenced interpretation, certain ideas can by synthesized. Integration of an appropriate testing program in the classroom with other elements of the educational process requires both kinds of interpretation. The teacher can get direction about which reference system to use by coordinating measurement interpretation with the instructional program. The thrust of teaching to mastery requires CRM, and teaching for the maximum requires NRM. The important factor to consider is not whether a test is a criterion-referenced test or a norm-referenced test but, rather, what frame of reference will be used for interpreting the scores on the test. In turn, the interpretation system to be used will direct the construction of the appropriate test items, difficulty levels of items, and other subtle differences.

The question is not so much about CRM and NRM but about the interpretation system to be used to give meaning to the student scores. One type of interpretation directs the teacher to CRM and construction of a test to measure a specific domain of minimum behaviors, and the other type of interpretation directs the teacher to NRM and construction of a test to measure a set of generally stated instructional objectives.

Glossary

Since this book on administration, scoring, and score interpretation is somewhat technical in nature, certain words may be new to the reader. Other commonly used words may take on a different meaning in this book. The meanings of selected words are denoted below. Words explained within the narrative of the book are not included. For a more complete explanation of other terms in measurement and evaluation, refer to the *Dictionary of Education*[1] and *Classroom Measurement and Evaluation*.[2]

Affective: The area of human action which emphasizes the internalized processes such as emotion, feeling, interest, attitude, value, character development, and motivation.

Answer sheet: A separate test page which the examinee uses to record the selected responses. Syn: response sheet.

Confidence interval: A range of possible values which has a particular probability of including a student's true score. As the probability is increased, the range of the confidence interval is increased. Likewise, if the probability is decreased, the interval set for confidence will decrease. The standard error of measurement is used to set a confidence interval for placement of the obtained score in relation to the student's **true score.**

---

[1] Carter V. Good, ed. *Dictionary of Education,* 3rd ed., (New York: McGraw-Hill Book Company, 1973.)

[2] Charles D. Hopkins and Richard L. Antes, *Classroom Measurement and Evaluation* (Itasca, Ill.: F. E. Peacock Publishers, Inc., 1978), pp. 414-33.

Descriptor set: A collection of ordered classes which establishes the degrees of worthiness of student performance. Used with criterion-referenced procedures.

Deviation: The numerical difference of a raw score from the mean of the distribution. $(X - \bar{X})$

Difficulty: The degree of arduousness of a test task for students as opposed to the easiness of the test task. Difficulty is measured by the **difficulty index (P_D).**

Difficulty index (P_D): A measure of the percentage of incorrect responses determined by dividing the number of students who got the item wrong by the number who tried the item. Used to establish how difficult an item was for the group who took the test. (See **Easiness index.**)

Direct observation: Noticing of phenomena without any intervening factor between the observer and that which is being observed. A record of the situation is made.

Discrimination: Ability of a true-false or multiple-choice item to make distinction between high- and low-scoring students based on the total test score. Discrimination is measured by the **discrimination index (D).**

Discrimination index (D): A value which indicates the ability of an item to separate high-achieving students from low-achieving students. The most commonly used index is obtained by comparing the number in the highest 27 percent of the group who responded correctly with the number in the lowest 27 percent who responded correctly.

Easiness index (P_E): A measure of the percentage of correct responses determined by dividing the number of students getting the item right by the number who tried the item. Used to establish how easy an item was for the group who took the test. (See **Difficulty index.**)

Evaluation: The continuous inspection of all available informaton concerning the student, teacher, educational program, and the teaching-learning process to ascertain the degree of change in students and to form valid judgments about the students and the effectiveness of the program.

Group formula: A rule which describes a way of proceeding to a solution using scores which have been collapsed into wide intervals.

Index: A number that is made up of two or more numbers. Ex: The Dow-Jones Average is an index of the price of several stocks.

Item analysis: An examination of student performance for each item on a test. It consists of reexamination of the responses to items of a test by applying mathematical techniques to assess two characteristics—**difficulty** and **discrimination**—of each objective item on the test.

Key: A solution set containing the correct responses to objective test items.

Norm: A value or set of values reflecting performances of a defined group on a test or inventory. Used in testing to aid in interpretation of scores on **standardized tests.**

Norm group: The set of subjects used to establish the averages to be used to interpret student scores on a **standardized test.**

Measurement: A process that assigns by rule a numerical description to observation of some attribute of an object, person, or event.

Problem-type Item: A challenging situation posed to a student which requires reflective thinking for solution in technical terms, or a mathematical task presented in algorithmic form.

Prescriptive learning: Instructional activities assigned from the diagnosis of specific needs of an individual. Usually a product of formative evaluation.

Psychological measurement: Quantification of hidden attributes of human subjects. It deals with the **measurement** and quantification of the factors of intelligence, emotions, and personality.

Psychomotor: The area of human action which emphasizes all types of body movements which are involuntary or voluntary.

Range: The difference in score units between the highest and lowest scores in a distribution. Range $= X_H - X_L$ [If the data are continuous and reported in units of one rather than fractions, the range can be defined as being equal to $(X_H - X_L + 1)$].

Raw score: The first score given to a test paper. It may include weighting and a correction for guessing, but no other transformation.

Reliability: Consistency of observation. The consistency with which a data-collection device measures whatever it is that the device measures. The degree of reliability may be reported as a correlation coefficient. It may be interpreted by the standard error of measurement.

Representative: The reflection of characteristics of something in something else. Syn: typical.

Sample: Any subset of persons or items selected to represent a larger group or population.

Selection-type Item: An item which requires the student to choose from provided alternatives.

Sounding board: Something that serves to reflect sound or to mirror ideas back to someone for consideration or reflection.

Standard: Anything, as a rule or principle, used as a basis for judgment.

Standardized test: A commercially printed test for which content has been selected and checked empirically. The test is standardized so that administration and scoring procedures are the same for all test takers. Score interpretation is made to averages of performances of groups of test takers whose scores are then used for making comparison to interpret obtained scores.

Sum of squares: $\Sigma(X - \bar{X})^2$. The total of the squares of the deviations of scores from the mean.

Supply-type Item: An item that requires the student to create a response within the structure provided by the item.

Table of specifications: A two-dimensional chart used to direct the writing of test items and construction of a test so that the subject topics and behaviors are emphasized in their relative degrees of importance as reflected by objectives and classroom emphasis.

Task: An assigned piece of work which describes what a test taker is to do. The expectation is clearly outlined by the test item.

Test-taking skill: Knowledge and experience of taking a test which assists the test taker in using test time wisely and to respond appropriately to items, as well as coping with other elements of the testing session.

Test-wise: When an individual has knowledge of clues about correct responses because of faults in the item. This knowledge enables the test taker to respond to items correctly when s/he does not know the correct answer.

Transformation: A systematic alteration in a set of scores or observations whereby certain characteristics of the set are changed and other characteristics remain unchanged. The operation by which the original or **raw scores** (X-values) can be converted into standard scores.

True score: An average of a very large number of possible scores that an individual could conceivably score on the administration of a test. The value of an observation entirely free from error. The mean of an infinite number of observations of a quantity.

Unit: A single, indivisible entity. A fixed quantity or amount. In testing, any specified amount or quantity to be counted to a composite test score.

Validity: The degree to which observation describes accurately what is being measured.

Variable: A property whereby the members of a group or set differ one from another. Any trait or characteristic which may assume different values for different subjects.

Variance: A measure of variability. The standard deviation value squared. A mean square obtained by squaring each score's deviation from the mean, summing and dividing by the number of scores.

.

Bibliography

Ahmann, J. Stanley and Marvin D. Glock. *Evaluating Pupil Growth.* 5th ed. Boston: Allyn and Bacon, Inc., 1975.

Anderson, Scarvia B., et al. *Encyclopedia of Educational Evaluation.* San Francisco: Jossey-Bass Publishers, 1975.

Bloom, Benjamin, S., et al. *Handbook on Formative and Summative Evaluation of Student Learning.* New York: McGraw-Hill Book Co., 1971.

Boehm, Anne E. *Boehm Test of Basic Concepts.* New York: Psychological Corporation, 1970.

Buros, Oscar K., ed. *Mental Measurements Yearbooks.* Highland Park, N.J.: Gryphon Press, 1938, 1940, 1949, 1953, 1959, 1965, 1972, 1978.

Buros, Oscar K., ed. *Tests in Print II.* Highland Park, N.J.: Gryphon Press, 1974.

Castaldi, Basil. *Creative Planning of Educational Facilities.* Chicago, Ill.: Rand McNally and Company, 1969.

Durost, W. N. *The Characteristics, Use, and Computation of Stanines.* New York: Harcourt, Brace, Jovanovich, Inc., 1961.

Ebel, Robert L. *Essentials of Educational Measurement.* Englewood Cliffs, N.J.: Prentice-Hall, Inc., 1972.

Good, Carter V., ed. *Dictionary of Education.* 3rd ed. New York: McGraw-Hill Book Co., 1973.

Gronlund, Norman E. *Measurement and Evaluation in Teaching.* 3rd ed. New York: The Macmillan Company, 1976.

Hambleton, Ronald K., et al. "Criterion-Referenced Testing and Measurement: A Review of Technical Issues and Developments." *Review of Educational Research* 48 (Winter 1978):3.

Hills, John R. *Measurement and Evaluation in the Classroom.* Columbus, Ohio: Charles E. Merrill Publishing Co., 1976.

Hopkins, Charles D. *Describing Data Statistically.* Columbus, Ohio: Charles E. Merrill Publishing Co., 1974.

Hopkins, Charles D. and Richard L. Antes. *Classroom Measurement and Evaluation.* Itasca, Ill.: F. E. Peacock Publishers, Inc., 1978.

Hopkins, Charles D. and Richard L. Antes. *Classroom Testing: Construction.* Itasca, Ill.: F. E. Peacock Publishers, Inc., 1979.

Lindquist, E. F., ed. *Educational Measurement.* Washington, D. C.: American Council on Education, 1951.

Noll, Victor H. and Dale P. Scannell. *Introduction to Educational Measurement,* 3rd ed. Boston: Houghton-Mifflin Co., 1972.

Popham, W. James. *Criterion-Referenced Measurement.* Englewood, Cliffs, N.J.: Prentice-Hall, Inc., 1978.

Standards of Educational and Psychological Tests and Manuals. Washington, D.C.: American Psychological Association, 1974.

Thorndike, Robert L., ed. *Educational Measurement.* 2nd ed. Washington, D.C.: American Council on Education, 1971.

"Writing Skills Lacking 'Essential Trio,'" *NAEP Newsletter.* Denver, Colorado: National Assessment of Educational Progress, October 1977.

Index

155

LB3051 .H7   010101 000
Hopkins, Charles D.
Classroom testing : administra

0 2002 0023039 5
YORK COLLEGE OF PENNSYLVANIA 17403